Walking the
Invisible Gemba

SAM YANKELEVITCH

My grandfather said: In business, people are
your most important asset.

My father said: In life, time is your most important asset.

My mother said: Go see for yourself,

and off she sent me on a journey into the invisible gemba.

Acknowledgements

MOST SINCERE APPRECIATION TO Mr. Franz Linner, BMW SVP of Supplier Networks NAFTA. Without his confidence, support, and promotion, the ideas written in this work could not have been thoroughly tested and validated.

Genuine thanks to Craig Long, a Performance Solutions by Milliken fellow, for his help affirming continuous improvement concepts and for continued encouragement on continuing the journey.

To my training partners, Brigitte Melzig and Marcel Sanchez, for making workshop facilitations a true learning experience. As a Colombian working with a Bavarian and a Cuban American, it made our work an exciting learning experience, moment by moment.

To Dr. Eric A. Hayler, for our conversations, his practical contributions, and for writing a very meaningful foreword, many, many thanks.

And to Leigh Ann Klaus, my copy editor, who was able to make sense of my manuscript and put it into proper English, which might help readers understand my message more clearly.

List of Sessions

Foreword

WHEN I INITIALLY ATTENDED AN American Society for Quality (ASQ) presentation by Sam Yankelevitch comparing communication to a process and using quality tools to improve the process, I was intrigued. In my work as a Lean Six Sigma Master Black Belt for BMW, I practice continuous improvement and problem solving daily. As an instructor of Lean Six Sigma Black Belt and Green Belt training, I tell my students that although many of the tools I teach originated in a manufacturing environment, they can be used for any kind of process. If communication is truly a process, then we should certainly be able to apply quality tools to improve communication. Anytime you're doing something, that's a process, whether or not you've thought about it that way. When you're making something, that's a manufacturing process. If there is an exchange of goods, services, or information, that's a transactional process. Communication is an example of a transactional process.

Continuous improvement, whether it's Lean Six Sigma or another discipline, is a collection of tools and methods. All are related and serve a similar purpose. In continuous improvement we are either looking to solve a problem, or seeking opportunities for improvement. One of the seven basic quality tools is the fishbone (Ishikawa) diagram. In a manufacturing environment it is typical to begin with the six Ms on the fishbone – Man, Method, Machine, Materials, Measurement, and Mother Nature. After thorough brainstorming, very often the Man branch of the fishbone diagram has the most ideas on it. Why? This is partly because so many potential sources of problems come from the behavior of people. Often soft skills are overlooked in favor of technical skills when people are selected and trained to perform a task. To influence changes in behavior, one must rely on personal and social motivation and ability, and at the core of this is communication.

In *Walking the Invisible Gemba*, Yankelevitch points out that culture, language, and environment are three key sources of variation. Culture can be national culture, regional culture, company culture, and even departmental culture. It's very difficult to understand how others see you through their own eyes. A few years ago, I made my first trip to the United Kingdom. I was attending a week-long training class with colleagues from my company who worked in various part of the country. I was the only American in the group. During my trip I noticed that over time I had acquired many misconceptions about the UK, the people there, and how they behave. I was glad to have the opportunity to be educated in this way. At one point I even asked someone if I would be understood better if I adopted an English accent. I gave them a few sentences in my best English accent, and they laughed. I was told that I used a mixture of several different regional accents and together it sounded odd. I was assured that my best chance to be understood was to use my normal American accent.

I became curious as to how I was perceived as an American. Since I grew up in the Northeast but lived for a number of years in the South, I wondered if my speech was a source of confusion for anyone. I asked several of my British colleagues to imitate me. No matter how hard I tried, I couldn't get any takers. I asked several of them to speak in an American accent, but they said they couldn't. Then, toward the end of the week, the group went out to dinner and then for drinks afterward. After several pints of Guinness, I finally managed to get one classmate to give it a try. He said, "How you doin?'" in his best New York accent a la Joey Tribbiani from the TV show *Friends*. It was my turn to laugh! An interesting stereotype.

In college I majored in chemistry. In graduate school, my specialty was inorganic chemistry, and I spent many hours in the lab working toward my thesis on solid state materials. Our lab group consisted of a number of students and post-doctoral fellows from all over the world. Having grown-up in central New Jersey in the 1970s, this was a new environment for me. For a while I struggled with communication. Our group had people from India, Taiwan, Japan, and Ethiopia. Many were new in the United States and spoke poor English. I spoke none of their native languages. In an attempt to be better understood, I tried speaking to them in the kind of broken English they used. This could sound disrespectful, but that was definitely not the intention. In fact, it almost worked. I found it was helpful when I used the same words in the context they did. What I learned quickly was that my speaking the same way did not work for everyone. For example, when our visiting professor from Japan wanted a Phillips head screwdriver, he would ask me for a "plus." If I needed a Phillips head, I could ask him for a "plus." However, if I asked for a "plus" from anyone else, they would not understand me.

Learning multiple forms of broken English was not particularly efficient or effective. In addition, when I gave a presentation to the entire group all I had was my normal speech. I decided I would learn to speak the clearest English that I could. As benchmarks, I chose the anchors of the national and local newscasts. I would watch and listen to Tom Brokaw, Chuck Scarborough, and others. I would repeat them line after line and try to mimic their accent, speed, intonation, and volume. This practice has served me well in a number of multicultural environments. These days most Americans have trouble identifying what part of the country I'm from by my speech. Occasionally people will guess that I'm from the Midwest, which is generally considered to be the most accent-neutral area of the country.

In my continuous improvement work I regularly facilitate various types of meetings and workshops. It's considered best practice to establish ground rules when starting to work with a new group. Over time I began to let this practice lapse when working with groups in my own company. I noticed that it was not necessary for us to agree on how we would handle interruptions like phone calls, needing to put devices on silent or vibrate, or what constitutes timely communication, because we all have been working in the same environment and we all have similar expectations. There was one very notable exception to this if I had anyone in the room from our IT area. Besides being physically separated from many of the rest of the company's working groups, they had a very different attitude toward technology and utilizing devices. Most people from our IT area would have their faces buried in their laptop screens during workshops and meetings. Many were typing away at what I initially assumed were emails or other work. I took this as a sign of disrespect and an impediment to the communication in our meeting. At this point I returned to my practice of establishing clear ground rules when working with a new group that included anyone from IT. What I learned later is that most of the IT people were actively working on our project work while they had their faces in their laptops. They began to feedback information regarding the work we were doing. I discovered many were taking notes in various electronic formats, a practice I have since adopted myself. These days I often return to the best practice of establishing ground rules, as I've recognized how important they are for those who are new to the company or for process partners who are coming from suppliers, vendors, or elsewhere outside our organization.

In thinking about communication as a process, we can look to apply the Lean Six Sigma methods and tools to improve processes. Problem-solving methods like PDCA (plan, do, check, act) or DMAIC (define, measure, analyze, improve, control) can be used to systematically identify sustainable solutions. We start by being clear about what the issue is and what we want the end result to look like. We look for the facts and data that describe our process and its key inputs. We look for all of the different things that could be contributing factors and analyze to find the ones that are the true root cause(s) of our problem. We come up with ideas to solve the root causes and select the ones that are not only the most effective, but also the actions that are the best for us. Finally, we put controls in place to make sure the problems don't return.

In this book, Sam describes how several basic continuous improvement tools such as fishbone diagrams and the 5 Whys can be applied to communication. In fact, many more such tools can be used. One that comes to mind is the SIPOC diagram. SIPOC stands for supplier, input, process, output, customer. It is a straight-forward tool used to scope the boundaries of a process, especially one that is not physical or cannot easily be seen. It is also a good starting point before creating a flowchart or value stream map. Notice that the center is input, process, output – a conventional view of a process. The customers receive the outputs and the suppliers provide the inputs. Once inputs and outputs are listed, it's a good exercise to list their measures, the Xs and Ys of the process.

Another Lean Six Sigma tool that can be adapted to the communication process is FMEA, which stands for failure mode and effects analysis. It is essentially a list of everything that can go wrong, prioritizing them based on severity, the probability of occurrence, and the likelihood of being detected. Then controls to mitigate the risk of these things happening are listed. The ideas for failure modes can come from the fishbone diagram. For simple communication processes, the task is not onerous. However, for complex communication processes, the list of potential errors can be quite long. Communications types of highest concern can be identified using a cause and effect matrix or another type of solution selection tool. The communication FMEA can be developed in the areas of highest concern.

Using these kinds of tools and methods is great for assisting work teams tasked with specific deliverables that work together regularly and have identifiable problems that need to be addressed. What can we do in less formal settings on a daily basis? The best practices that are used in team settings can work well and be applied more universally. Speaking clearly by slowing speech, reducing accents, consciously choosing easy-to-interpret words, minimizing jargon, and clearly defining acronyms in advance work in almost every setting.

Understanding that quality is everyone's responsibility is a pillar of a culture of quality. Understanding that effective communication is everyone's responsibility is a pillar of a culture of communication. Culture can be thought of as a collection of the things you do when no one is watching. A culture of communication supports a culture of quality. A culture of quality supports success.

January 2018

Dr. Eric A. Hayler
Lean Six Sigma Master Black Belt, BMW
Past Chair of the Board of Directors, ASQ

"We must always keep in mind that the greatest waste is waste we do not see."

Shigeo Shingo (1987)

Preamble and Introduction

BY THE TIME I HEARD the word *gemba*, and the concept it represented back then, I had already experimented with many of the ideas and methodologies proposed in the few books and manuals published in the mid-1980s and early 1990's ([1]). There were no sensei available and no consultants. This, in retrospect, was the best thing that could have happened.

Trial and error and learning by doing were the only ways we could prove whether the case studies and explanations from the books would actually work. In addition, the key ideas presented in *The Goal* (Goldratt and Cox 1986) served as a foundation to deeply challenge what I had learned about processes and manufacturing during my studies in industrial engineering.

In the mid-1980s I was in charge of a lock and hardware manufacturing facility in Colombia where batch processes ruled and inventories were deemed assets, conveniently helping to hide processing problems. This was all low-hanging fruit that allowed me and my team to see real potential for improvement in quality and efficiency.

Trial and error worked quite well, and the processes we selected to improve achieved immediate gains. These gains translated into opportunities to compete in the international arena and grow our sales. They also provided an opportunity to travel to other continents to establish relationships with customers, and with suppliers of the equipment, tooling, and materials needed to transform and grow the company even more.

This is where I first became aware of hidden processes – invisible acts that impact our work. In my first encounters with global suppliers from Spain, China, Japan, Mexico, Italy, Malaysia, and other countries, small misunderstandings led to frustration and highly undesirable costs.

Even after sending samples, drawings, and specifications of components to component suppliers or tool builders – often via surface mail – we would receive counter samples and products that did not match what we tried to communicate in our requests.

It took a lot of back-and-forth interaction between the plant and the supplier to match the original requirements, and miscommunication started to surface as a real issue.

Coincidentally, when miscommunication happened locally inside the four walls of our plant, we did not give it the attention it deserved. Looking back, I now recognize the missed opportunity of taking care of every non-value-added activity while it's still small. Tackling problems as they arise is indeed a good practice, considering immediate countermeasures might be simpler to implement.

Interestingly, another realization came about: organizational problems related to miscommunication seldom came from lack of technical skills for solving problems. Instead, most of the problems were caused by a lack of understanding of how to interact adequately with other humans, locally and globally.

Although everyone believed they were communicating, they were actually doing it poorly, inadvertently generating problems, and then blaming others.

Fast forward to the 21ˢᵗ century.

In 2002, a new challenge came about as I took a position as vice president and general manager of a German-based automotive company in South Carolina. One of my main responsibilities was to bring lean thinking into an operation that was based on batch processing and layouts founded on equipment efficiencies. Transformation had to be achieved in a multicultural environment where German engineers had to work together with Americans from South Carolina, and a Latin American.

While we were able to implement a robust lean program on the factory floor, unfortunately the philosophy did not extend to the whole enterprise, and many of the gains we achieved were erased because of simple misunderstandings and cultural complications.

Proof of this became evident when we performed systemic root cause analysis, which directly exposed how communication and culture were responsible for lost customer contracts and profits. Consequently, the hidden sources of waste were made visible.

In 2013, after I left the industry, I started a new journey with the idea of applying lean and quality thinking to improve the process of communication. Once I realized that the place where the action happens is not necessarily the shop floor as we know it, the meaning of the word gemba started to transform.

The factories I'm involved with are no longer collections of machines lined up from dock to stock. Instead, they look more like webs of interconnected functions represented by teams of people who need to communicate effectively. Supply chains are in fact factories where value has to be added in each link, just like on a manufacturing floor.

This is the context of the new gemba, the invisible one.

When I published *Lean Potion #9: Communication: The Next Lean Frontier* (Yankelevitch 2014), I proposed the use of lean methodologies such as 5S and standard work, and a first stab at PDCA (plan, do, check, act), to improve communication and reduce misunderstandings.

The premise was that before we get anything done physically, we have to communicate in order to coordinate our efforts.

Many of the stories and cases mentioned in that book came from experiences of waste and quality defects triggered by uncontrolled human processes that either I or my colleague, Claire Kuhl, witnessed in diverse industries.

Since then, I have co-facilitated numerous workshops and seminars on adopting lean thinking and quality concepts in situations where factors such as culture, language, and distance were obvious direct contributors to time wasted, project delays and late deliveries, and many quality problems.

In numerous conferences and articles, I've provided ways to use concepts such as standard work, Jidoka, do it right the first time, and PDCA to improve the process of communication.

Now, with a higher degree of confidence, I continue to support leaders and teams who are aligned with these ideas.

Yes, there is a way to adopt lean thinking to improve communication in organizations.

I recently revisited a story from Shigeo Shingo where he states:

".... real waste lurks in forms that do not look like waste ... we must keep in mind the greatest waste is waste we do not see" (Shingo 1987).

Since the time of that writing, businesses have become more complex and the risks have increased, due in large part to our globally interlinked organizations, where there can be significant suffering even from a small misunderstanding.

It has become clear now that there are no big problems, only a constellation of small, unnoticed ones that creep silently into our processes. Communication is one of those processes.

Enter Mr. Onata.

In *Global Lean: Seeing the New Waste Rooted in Communication, Distance, and Culture* (Yankelevitch 2016), Mr. Kami Onata appears as the Japanese sensei who provides a German-based company with valuable countermeasures to offset its very costly and disastrous entry into the global arena.

And because Mr. Onata is such a character, literally, he returns in this book to share his perspective on the hidden forces we cannot see but keep impacting our operations and our results. By bringing these invisible factors to the surface, he offers a complementary way to use lean and quality thinking toward a more holistic approach to continuous improvement.

According to Mr. Onata, there are *Goryō* lurking in the shadows of our processes – vengeful ghosts that are waiting to pounce on our operations, wreaking havoc and chaos while adding to the uncontrolled variation.

Even if you can't see them, the Goryō are there, hurting our results.

This book is an invitation to you from Mr. Onata to join him in the journey of improvement in nontraditional processes. By paying more attention to the invisible gemba, the place where every interaction occurs intended to trigger a physical activity, our organizations will stand a better chance of surviving and thriving in this very complex and interconnected world.

Let's not practice limited continuous improvement; if there is waste, it's still our responsibility to fix it.

"Contemplate a difficulty when it is easy. Manage a great thing when it is small ..."

Tao Te Ching

Just because we cannot see things that are invisible does not mean they have no impact on our operations and results. Despite all the technology we have successfully developed, our human brains are still limited in many ways, preventing us from noticing things that contribute to problems, even though the same problems repeat over and over.

The way we think about quality and continuous improvement is often constrained by the way we have been programmed. To be clear, it's not the "way" that is the issue;

rather, it is how this limits us from using the same ideas and methodologies to help reduce problems caused by factors we barely notice yet are common causes of so many difficulties in organizations.

We are so focused on the physical and tangible activities that our attention is spent on these, while other things go unnoticed. Besides, we may think that if we do focus too much on something else, we will not have time to complete our tasks.

For some continuous improvement professionals, the stigma of the word *manufacturing*, as it is associated with the concept of *lean manufacturing*, can act as a limiting factor when it focuses heavily on solving issues related to the manufacturing shop floor, thus leaving out other areas.

Sustaining 5S and keeping an eye out for the seven wastes, for example, can keep us overly engrossed in these activities, detracting from a much-needed emphasis on other important sources of waste.

While visual management is a great concept to show immediately how a process is trending and where physical problems lie, at the same time it draws our attention away from non-physical sources of waste.

Similarly, we tend to think of quality as meeting the material specifications of a product, preventing physical defects from getting to our customers. This is important, of course, but it causes us to miss hidden contributing factors.

A notorious influencer we seldom take responsibility for as quality and continuous improvement specialists is *miscommunication* considering the impact it has on our physical processes.

While we cannot *see* communication, we do experience the results of *miscommunication*.

Even though this is not a process we are accustomed to dealing with using our skillsets, it is imperative that we begin to take responsibility, considering the circumstances have changed, and continue to change faster, with ever more complexity and risk to our operations.

This book offers the opportunity for quality and continuous improvement professionals to use our knowledge and take on the problems that misunderstandings have caused in our organizations, with our customers, and with our suppliers.

Clearly, miscommunication is nothing new. As humans we have always needed to communicate with each other to get things done, sometimes for the survival of our tribe. When we were in smaller groups, working closely in the same location, communication was taken for granted. It did not stand out as a problem, possibly because misunderstandings could be caught and corrected very quickly.

We could say that cause and effect were close in time and space.

Misunderstandings were solved quickly, and, therefore, we paid little attention to communication as a source of waste, and instead decided to focus on physical issues.

The world, however, has changed, and with a globalized economy, interconnected by technologies that our human brains have not fully developed to engage with, we have forgotten that humans are still on the front lines – and that we need to communicate to ensure the customer is served.

Manufacturing, for example, no longer happens exclusively inside four walls. Process steps are dispersed, apart from one another, sometimes physically separated by thousands of miles and multiple time zones.

Similarly, suppliers are not always close by, and the distance in between impacts the effectiveness of doing business. Customers are also spread across the globe, and it can be difficult to fully understand their fleeting tastes and expectations, which have accelerated in the way they continuously renovate, making these a moving target.

The speed of things has pushed many of us into a senseless multitasking environment, where we mistakenly believe we are accomplishing more, but are actually overwhelming our minds so we cannot dedicate our attention to anything specific or listen for more than a tiny fraction of time.

Multitasking has become the standard way to work; it is a big factor that further contributes to miscommunication, while at the same time helping to conceal it, making it even more difficult to detect and solve.

Why now?

Although *globalization* has created the need to function in a more coordinated way, we don't always follow suit. And while it's true that we have great technologies to allow us to connect better, we are not necessarily coordinating better.

Sometimes it takes an exaggeration to make the invisible visible. This is the case when people are trying to get things done right in multiple languages, or with many time zones in between, which helps highlight a core process we have been missing or dodging.

If we consider the increased level of interdependence, it encourages us to fully accept that we must interact with more people more frequently to get things done. Consequently, if we want to get things done right the first time, we have to learn how to interact effectively.

One thing globalization has helped emphasize is the importance of communication.

In order to get anything done when more than one person is involved, we first have to communicate a request, an expectation, or an instruction in a way such that everyone understands it the same. Such interactions are meant to help coordinate tasks and activities so things follow a certain path toward a specific goal.

"Communication is everyone's job."

Communication is the essential component in a human interaction that is intended to drive actions and tasks. It is an activity in and of itself, and it happens before physical actions, before things get done.

In any case, if we are not effective communicators within our organization, now is the time to bring this process to the surface and improve it so its potential impact – both positive and negative – on our physical processes can be better controlled.

SAM YANKELEVITCH

At the same time, we have reached critical mass to a point where thousands of professionals have knowledge and experience in quality and continuous improvement, which enables a greater group of people to start approaching the core process of communication with a structured mindset and a robust set of methodologies and tools.

The thinking has expanded into many other sectors outside traditional manufacturing such as healthcare, banking, and construction.

Communication is not the responsibility of one area in an organization. Realistically, the human resources (HR) department is not in charge of this process, nor is this topic exclusive for external consultants or business coaches to support.

If "Quality control is everyone's job," (Feigenbaum 1983), then the time has come for communication to be everyone's job.

Furthermore, continuous improvement is meant to scrutinize every activity in every process of an organization to determine where value is not being added and waste or defects can materialize. By choosing to focus only on certain things could mean we are practicing limited continuous improvement. Therefore, this choice is also greatly responsible for the recurring problems our organizations experience.

Complexity is on the rise and working inside complex systems typically involves having to get more things done within the same limited amount time. If we consider that in business we have to communicate before anything gets done, then it makes sense to set the goal of getting our messages across in a way that everyone involved is on the same page.

There are three key points about communication that will be unraveled throughout this book:

1. Communication is invisible - we cannot see it, but it does impact our results.

2. Communication is a process - we are good at dealing with processes.

3. Communication precedes action - it is the source of coordinated physical actions.

This book is about bringing communication to the surface so we can become truly aware of its contribution to many of the problems our organizations face today. It's about making the invisible visible.

It's an invitation to the quality and continuous improvement community to take notice and begin to use our skills toward reducing and removing its negative effects.

If we want to remain competitive and grow in the new global workplace, getting things done right the first time must be complemented to include the process of communication, especially if it's a precursor to physical activities.

This book is intended to help readers grasp, feel, and see the true nature of our interactions; the risk and impact these have on our operations; and the responsibility we must own if we are really committed to continuous improvement.

Because there are many ideas on approaching this topic toward solutions, there is no one-size-fits-all magic formula to solve complexity.

Therefore, it's not written in a prescriptive way.

Instead, it will provide you, the reader, with ideas and ways to complement your skills and help you escape a habituated attention force that blinds us and keeps us from going deeper into our continuous improvement journey. (South Carolina, December 2017)

How the book flows

The book flows via a series of presentations at a conference led by Kami Onata, the character sensei who first appeared in *Global Lean: Seeing the New Waste Rooted in Communication, Distance, and Culture* (Yankelevitch 2016), where he helped Boern Industries realize the impact of invisible factors on its operations and its results.

Mr. Onata's discussions begin with his explanation about the origins of the word gemba and the changes that have happened at the gemba.

Then, in session 2, he expresses a sense of urgency for organizations and the new risks posed on our processes by factors related to globalization.

In session 3, Mr. Onata brings to light how we tend to choose some wastes over others, and how this is a problem in the current state of business.

Sessions 4 and 5 are dedicated to the heightened importance of interdependence and the interactions needed between the people responsible for process steps that are separated physically.

In session 6, Mr. Onata brings up the three barriers that are getting in the way of flow and affecting execution.

Session 7 establishes responsibility in the organization for the invisible factors that cause problems in our organizations, and in session 8 he shows us some problem-solving ideas adapted from lean and quality to find solutions for such factors.

Additional cases are presented in session 9 to show how some teams have applied the concepts, and a short list of points is summarized in a conclusion in session 10.

Each session presents a series of questions to Mr. Onata asked by the attendees at the conference. These are intended to further explore the opportunities the new gemba has snuck into our processes and supply chains.

"Quality begins when everybody in the organization commits to never sending rejects or imperfect information to the next process."

Masaaki Imai (1997)

Session 1

Mr. Onata's Invisible Gemba

CONFERENCE ANNOUNCER: THANK YOU for coming this morning to the International Conference of Quality in Operations. Today we are very fortunate to have Mr. Kami Onata, who will be presenting on the topic of how to improve communication through the use of lean and quality thinking. The title of his conference today is "Walking the Invisible Gemba."

While Mr. Onata participated in several improvement processes in Japan, Europe, and the Americas, for the past few years he has applied and promoted a way to complement our traditional lean thinking by including activities we often pay less attention to than perhaps we should.

To keep this presentation running on time, we ask that you wait until Mr. Onata prompts us to ask questions, and he will gladly answer them for you. Mr. Onata will often be available during breaks, and he will probably sit and have lunch with you, so you may look for him and get your questions answered.

Please welcome Mr. Onata. We hope you enjoy and learn from him today.

Mr. Onata: Good morning everyone.

The term *gemba* has been widely adopted in continuous improvement circles to represent the factory floor and also "where the real activity is happening."

Mr. Masaaki Imai, who first brought this concept from Japan for the benefit of the rest of the world, talked about the gemba as "the workplace where activities happen that either add value, or not" (Imai 1997).

Going to the gemba, or walking the gemba, is the practice of *going to see* activities at the physical place where they are occurring, with the intention of witnessing and directly observing reality, while avoiding opinions or cold data from spreadsheets. At that place we will be looking at the value being added, from the customer's perspective.

When I was younger, I remember watching TV with my father, and the announcer would use the word "gemba" when he was reporting something from "the scene of the crime," meaning where the action was occurring.

Today, however, this definition is somewhat problematic, not because the meaning of the word has changed, but because the scene of the crime has changed. It's like in *The Wizard of Oz* when Dorothy said to her dog, "Toto, I've a feeling we're not in Kansas anymore." (MGM 1939)

The days of more comfortable surroundings, of working with people who speak our language and share the same values, have changed dramatically, and continue to change at an accelerated pace.

The context of today's business world is far different than when the term *gemba* was originally adopted, although the thinking behind the concept is still great. However, I believe the way we use it needs to be readapted to the current reality for it to truly serve its purpose.

If we choose not to accept that circumstances have changed, then going to a gemba that shows only a partial reality is confirmation that we are committed to practicing limited continuous improvement.

This is not going to help our organizations survive in the current reality.

Let me explain.

When we talk about business today, the word *globalization* is often a part of the discussion because of the rapid acceleration of this phenomenon that has shaken, and continues to shake, the foundations of numerous organizations.

For those who take this factor lightly, be warned that this is not just a platitude; it has already caused a radical impact on the way much business is done today.

Globalization actually means that what was local and close is now distanced, and the people who have to coordinate and synchronize the activities required to deliver value to the customer are not only separated physically, but also distanced by their unique and diverse world views.

Or just look at the extended supply chains, where each process step is only a portion of the total steps needed to serve a customer.

If the physical activities are dispersed, how might we go to observe reality and gather facts about what is really happening? How can we walk that gemba?

Said differently, the scene of the crime has today become a really, really big area, making it difficult to physically see every single process, activity, or motion.

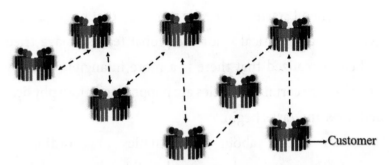

Today's factories are made up of interdependent teams that are not necessarily inside four walls. The teams are interconnected in order to serve a customer.

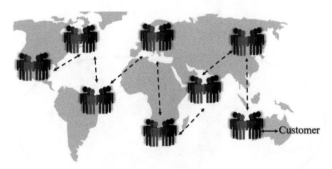

Some interconnected factories are dispersed across many continents and time zones.

Before I walked on stage, I spoke to some of you in the audience, and you asked me to explain a bit about the title of my presentation. I suppose it is somewhat curious.

OK. So here it goes: Even though we cannot see things that are invisible does not mean those things are not affecting the work we do and how we get things done.

So, when I started to see the problems that became quite evident – and critical – for the global teams I have tried to help, I realized that there is a more intangible "factory floor" where certain activities are happening before physical activities and tasks begin.

I am talking about the activities of coordination and synchronization between the different areas of an organization, as they attempt to get things done, to take care of the expectations of the customer.

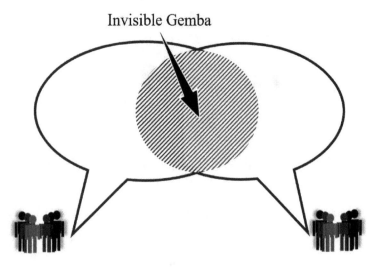

Invisible Gemba

The place where interactions happen that trigger the physical activities required to satisfy the customer.

It's about the interactions needed to organize all the physical tasks between people and systems from every area.

The new scene of the crime happens at the intersection you see on the screen, where instructions, requests, and expectations are exchanged. And because we have become more interdependent on others to get things done and satisfy the customer, this intersection is very important.

This area here, this intersection, is what I refer to as the "invisible gemba." This is where my meaning and your meaning need to match to create value for the customer.

Now, what you see on the screen is only a model, but while the effects and results of an interaction are tangible, the actual activity that is happening is not. It is an invisible process –and this is why I chose to call it the "invisible gemba."

Therefore, the invisible gemba can also be interpreted as the place where interactions happen that trigger the physical activities required to satisfy the customer.

So, if the interactions don't go so well, what can we expect from the physical actions that follow?

The team members on the left are requesting a rabbit, but will most likely receive a duck.

We have to be able to see these activities as well; otherwise, what happens at the gemba stays at the gemba.

"...there is nothing more important for transaction of business than use of operational definitions. It could also be said that no requirement of industry is so much neglected."

W. Edwards Deming (1986)

Last week I was visiting my old friend Johannes Boern, the CEO of Boern Industries in Germany. (²)

We were recalling how a misunderstanding between his engineers in Germany and some colleagues in the United States and China triggered the loss of a very important contract from a key customer.

When they did a root cause analysis to learn from their mistake, they realized that a series of small misunderstandings made up the source of a very big impact to their bottom line.

And Johannes has since made a very important change by making it clear that it is everyone's responsibility to ensure exact, unambiguous, and clear communication in every area of the company.

I will expand on this concept later in my presentation.

Now, because I've stated the magic word *communication,* and I know that a monologue is dangerous, it may be a good time to ask for your reflections and questions. Do you have any so far?

Attendee 1: *Mr. Onata, I am a quality manager, and I want to know a bit more about your idea of communication. How does it tie into the work I do in my organization? Can you please orient me a little?*

Mr. Onata: Yes, thank you for your question. I'll open with a quote often attributed to Dr. W. Edwards Deming: "Quality is everyone's responsibility." ([3])

And I say: communication is everyone's responsibility.

Interactions are activities that happen between two or more players in a critical chain, and for the purpose of this conference, the focus is on the interactions intended to produce a tangible, measurable result.

At the core of an interaction is *communication*.

Communication lies at the source of any interaction required to get things done, and I mentioned globalization because it has heightened the level of importance. We cannot avoid it if we want to truly reduce and remove all potential waste from our physical processes.

The good thing is we have the knowledge and the tools to do this.

After all, if communication is a process, why would we not approach it with the same quality mindset we use in our continuous improvement journeys? Later I will show you some simple fishbone diagrams and 5 Whys that you can adopt to help you do so.

Considering that we have become extremely interdependent on others to get things done, our success now depends on others, and we must first communicate with others to coordinate tasks and activities; if we miscommunicate, the required tasks will not get done on time, may get done incorrectly, or perhaps not get done at all.

I hope this answers your question.

Attendee 2: *Mr. Onata, it sounds like things have accelerated quite a bit, maybe become more complex. You mentioned the work with Boern in Germany. Is there some general advice, or are there some suggestions you imparted to them that you can share so we can benefit from them?*

Mr. Onata: In the case of Boern industries, we focused on the urgency of adapting continuous improvement to the new reality, with the same energy we used on the manufacturing processes.

Check your current circumstances to see if it is indispensable to adjust your continuous improvement efforts to include any and all factors that have crept into your day-to-day execution, especially if you have teams involved in the extended value chain, interacting with suppliers and customers.

The fact that the world is interconnected should sound an alarm bell in any organization that intends to survive and thrive in this type of economy. Chances are there is an existing methodical and organized strategy to drive continuous improvement in your company.

Many organizations that have embedded lean or Six Sigma principles into their processes can fine-tune their work by including things that were not critical in the past. Knowing that the new circumstances have changed the name of the game, and heightened the impact of factors previously not deemed important, requires a change to the way we look at continuous improvement.

This means taking a fresh look at every activity that is necessary to create value for the end customer and not limit improvement efforts to traditional physical activities. What is required is an enterprise-wide effort that includes the effectiveness of the connections and interactions with all direct and indirect partners.

Ignoring and not adapting to the known changes is not only by definition waste, but also a strategic error that will make your chances of success much dimmer.

This may be a good moment to clarify another fact about the process of communication; that is, before anything gets done in a coordinated way, communication has to happen. Stated differently, communication precedes action.

And to be very clear, because communication precedes action, we should take this process very seriously in our continuous improvement efforts.

"The single biggest problem
in communication is the illusion
that it has taken place."

George Bernard Shaw

Please look at this quote attributed to Mr. George Bernard
Shaw where he states, "The single biggest problem
in communication is the illusion that it has taken place."
We will be addressing this illusion in this talk. The word
communication comes from the same source as *common*.

Until we have a common understanding, you and I will
not have communicated. We will just have the illusion that
we did.

My assistant is signaling that it's time for a 15-minute
break. Thank you. See you in 15! Don't be late.

"What happens at the gemba
stays at the gemba."

The Paradox of the New Gemba

MR. ONATA: WE ARE BACK. Did you have a chance to communicate with each other during the break? Perhaps you tried – the question is did communication really happen?

(Laughter)

Ladies and gentlemen, let's talk about something I call the paradox of the new gemba. It has to do with speed and our obsession with getting everything done quickly.

Here is what I mean by this:

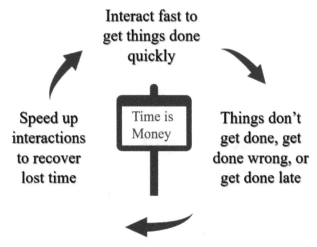

The paradox of the new gemba keeps things going too fast for us to see how we continuously create our own chaos.

While the need for speed in business is associated to the value "time is money," the need for coordination is now more challenging than ever before. Considering that coordination depends on the successful interactions between players in each value-adding step, if we look for speed in an interaction, we are risking a negative result for the physical action it is intended to trigger.

Herein lies an interesting paradox: when we are interacting, we may have to slow down in order to move fast. [4]

In this context, slowing down means taking the necessary time to establish clarity at the beginning of the process. It means ensuring zero ambiguity in setting an expectation for performance, and avoiding the unwanted, uncontrolled results of multiple interpretations.

Therefore, please ensure your organization is adapting to the new circumstances. It is important if you want to survive and thrive. OK?

It's truly amazing to me the level of sophistication in the technology we humans have developed and the speed at which things are happening. I am even more amazed, however, to see how we have not *really* learned the true nature of communication, and we don't naturally associate that gap with some grave consequences.

It's about cause and effect, ladies and gentlemen. Poor communication can cause poor execution.

And things are not so simple any more.

For sure, globalization has pushed us to develop better, more effective tools to communicate with partners across the globe. Although there are great new technologies to help us exchange messages with others, miscommunication is still rampant. Even information technology (IT) systems trying to communicate with other IT systems have interface problems that keep thousands of programmers and troubleshooters very busy. Last week I visited a production planning department where people were manually downloading data from their very expensive SAP system into spreadsheets. (^{5})

Then they were running calculations on the spreadsheets and uploading back into the SAP program. What a waste!

One could say that overdependency on technology is a bad side effect of the new gemba.

We love to use technology because it is a physical device that is tangible and perceivable. It's also a way for organizations to pretend they are solving the problems caused by miscommunication, and some have made IT the biggest part of their continuous improvement strategy.

Sure, IT definitely has its place, but so do humans, who must still interact daily so extended value chains can deliver products and services to their customers. And these humans, in many instances, face distance, cultural, and language obstacles to good communication.

These factors must be taken as seriously as other tangible issues. These factors increase the variation on our physical processes, and like Dr. Deming said: "Uncontrolled variation is the enemy of quality" (Kang and Kyam 2012).

It's interesting how when we are going to invest in a brand-new facility, a manufacturing process, or an IT system, the level of awareness for physical assets is usually very high. What I'm saying is that we should pay equal attention to these less tangible factors, because they can and will "kick our butts."

Now let me get back to the concept of the gemba.

One key benefit of walking the gemba is that cause and effect can be witnessed right at the source. Said differently, one can observe the results and the reasons for the results.

Unfortunately, when process steps are not close to each other, this distance makes the problem even worse, because it makes it difficult or even impossible to *go see* directly.

I think this is one of the less appreciated negative side effects of globalization, outsourcing, and working in an extended supply chain.

In such settings, cause and effect can happen with long intervals of time and space in between, making us lose our sense of the relationship between one and the other. Then, when we have negative results, we tend to make incomplete assessments, jump to conclusions, and decide on correctives that only last until the next time the problem repeats.

What is always visible, however, is the red ink on our profit and loss statements, due to the costs associated with repeat issues. Unfortunately, these bad costs are often taken for granted as costs of doing business in the new gemba.

In manufacturing you would see premium freight, quality spills and sorting, rework, and heroes flying across the globe to solve problems. This is certainly not a sustainable way to work, plus the losses incurred steal resources from opportunities for growing and achieving increased efficiencies.

Furthermore, if actions that can prevent the recurrence of such problems are not set in place, there is a real risk to the long-term strategy and the survival of the organization.

Here is an example: A large U.S. manufacturing company focused heavily on its processing know-how and expertise when it decided to transfer part of its assembly operations to the Ukraine. The company calculated hefty cost savings that would help it stay competitive.

Even though some executives highlighted the importance of working on language and culture, and developing their employees to support the new circumstances, for the transfer they only paid lip service to these factors and did not really invest the attention or the funds.

This company's competence was in its physical processes and not so much on people processes.

Company executives had estimated their benefit based on a six-month equipment transfer and ramp up. However, the actual time it took was 18 months, and when they did start operations, there were weekly crisis management meetings because the situation became more chaotic – lots of disasters, lots of emergencies. The impact to quality and delivery came at a very high cost – the company lost an important customer, as well as its longstanding reputation.

And the worst part: the company's brand was tarnished.

Only then, as a corrective action, did this company start to train key personnel about cultural differences that can affect their operations, and how to bridge the differences and align everyone. The company is also now driving a strong technical English learning initiative for the Ukrainian colleagues, to reduce the problems created by misunderstandings related to language.

This simplified story can help all of you as a "lesson learned" to avoid big losses.

I would also like to add something more about speed. After working for so many years in the United States, I noticed a difference in how most people here act as compared to my experience in the East.

Getting from point A to point B as fast as possible is the norm; that is, to arrive at point B the sooner the better. This suggests we are moving through the space in between without paying attention. We are impatient to arrive at our destination.

Perhaps in the past you rushed through, but I can tell you that in the new gemba, what lies along the way is very important. The real place is what is right in front of you, right now. That is your focus, not point B.

OK. Now as I did before, this is a good time to open the floor to your feedback, questions, or additional insight.

Attendee 3: *Hello, Mr. Onata-San. I work at a large OEM, and I am an engineer, part of a development team. Although we have a central development team, we depend on many other global players and often get hit with some of the issues you mentioned. The problem is our management likes to solve problems by force, usually sending teams of experts to fix things across continents. There is little effort to really understand the source of the issues. How do you see this? How can this be handled?*

Mr. Onata: Yes, I have been in such situations. We call in those "heroes" to solve problems when there is a crisis. The directive is to do whatever it takes to get the situation fixed. Remember that many organizations live quarterly, so that is what these experts are trained to do. They also get a pat on the back, because the immediate results are tangible. Problems are fixed – for the moment.

But when things repeat over and over, it's usually because only the point of cause has been addressed, but not the source, the origin of the problem. By the way, usually it is a combination of sources that causes the problems. And, in my experience dealing with heroes, they often like to fixate on just one thing, for a limited time. This will not lead to sustainable solutions.

"We can be heroes just for one day."

(Bowie and Eno 1977)

Here's what I have also encountered. When management knows that there are issues related to culture or language, they delegate these to other areas, typically their HR department.

I think everyone here realizes that preventive actions are usually better than corrective actions. The problem is that preventive actions may not always offer a guarantee that things will improve. So, managers may not take the risk to invest in them.

However, leaders who try to grasp the connection between miscommunication and tangible results are the ones who will not hesitate to make this a priority in their strategy.

My message to you is to give it an honest try. Use PDCA. Plan. Do. Check. Act. ([6])

If we don't try, we will never know, right?

Someone else please?

Attendee 4: *Hello, Mr. Onata. Thank you for speaking to us today. Our company was recently acquired by another, larger company. Originally, our directives and goals came from our U.S. headquarters, but each facility was allowed to lead the continuous improvement effort based on the local realities. But now, the company that acquired us from Spain is requiring us to follow one and only one way, their way, toward continuous improvement. The problem is that not only are people demotivated, but there are also things that worked well in Spain within the Spanish system that don't work in the United States. Really, the biggest issue we see is that we are not listening to each other's views and, at the end, the organization suffers. Have you experienced this, and how does it tie into the topic of communication? I'm sorry for such a long question.*

Mr. Onata: Well, sir, you just stated, "We are not listening to each other," so this is a very big barrier in the process of communication because there is no dialogue. I have actually detected this cultural problem before, and it comes up as a systemic root cause, when we drill deep into the problems. A solution to this can only happen via real dialogue, which also means listening to each other. In your case, I also suspect there is a feeling from the company that acquired yours that the way things were done at your facility was not good enough. What probably did not happen is a robust due diligence method before the acquisition. Their focus was limited to the visible – the physical assets.

By that I mean we must not only focus on the balance sheet, profit and loss, and physical processes and resources, but also the people side of the business. We need to examine the existing values and norms, so a plan can be established to work on a transition, integration, and then alignment. There is just so much waste when teams in the same organization are not aligned.

I hope that helps. Someone else?

Attendee 5: *Hi, I am enjoying your talk, but I am concerned with the way our organizations work, and we work inside them, so sometimes we cannot make the change. What can you suggest so we can make the point in such a way to start driving change even at the top?*

Mr. Onata: Sounds like a David and Goliath story. Well, it is kind of because we have some very engrained ways of working together. Sometimes it is tough because of the way we learned to do things without really knowing why. But we stick to our ways and defend them.

What I know is the same in every organization is how much one dollar is worth. So, if every dollar has the same value, then every activity should come under our scrutiny when there is potential for waste.

Every human interaction could cost us a dollar or more. Plus, a small misunderstanding can lead to a loss of more than a dollar. What I'm saying is that even the people at the top can understand the responsibility of taking on every activity that poses a risk to the organization.

In the case of quality and continuous improvement, it is possible we are trying to use someone else's way of approaching problems, as a way to fix our own. We are looking for a cookie-cutter way to fix things, when in reality every situation is different and demands a fresh analysis.

I am getting ahead of the next session, where I will share with you the idea of zero-base thinking, which is not only a great influencer, but also an effective way to ensure communication is taken seriously by everyone.

So, I think part of the answer for you will become a bit clearer in our next session.

Thank you for your question.

OK, let's paradox. Is that a verb?

Let's take a 10-minute break, so our brains can absorb and rest a bit, and then we can expand the topic for further understanding.

How Zero Helps to See the Invisible

Welcome back.

LAST WEEK I WAS VISITING one of my clients, and I presented a proposal for some workshops he wanted me to facilitate. My client acted very surprised with my proposal, and he told me he did not have enough in his budget to pay for the workshops.

I knew that he had to urgently fly in components at the last minute and scrap a large number of parts. These were repeat issues that were never actually resolved, but point to misunderstood instructions.

So, I asked my client, "How is it that you don't have a budget for external advice on how to reduce costs and, more important, achieve sustainable solutions, but you always come up with money to pay for blunders you can't explain?

This happens when we decide what gets measured and what does not. Budgets, for example, are wonderful devices for doing that, and, consequently, they help bury sources of waste – out of sight, out of mind.

Do you have this in your company?

Are your budgets helping to keep wasteful activities invisible?

In a sense, when we budget for certain things, we are giving ourselves random allowances to continue with wasteful activities somewhere else in the company. Not only does this practice go against continuous improvement, but it also blinds us when we see our performance has improved compared to the budget, and the company is satisfied, proclaiming "improvement" has been obtained.

Therefore, limiting our improvement to a budget prevents us from seeing different critical opportunities that might be contributing to high unwanted costs.

In addition, I think companies that choose to blindly follow ideas based on Toyota's principles, such as the seven wastes, will also miss other sources of waste that are present and, therefore, will not be able to address those sources because their continuous improvement is moving inside a limited scope.

In summary, while budgets move people toward a random number, true continuous improvement should move people toward zero tolerance.

We all have a zero-defect policy, don't we?

Therefore, the idea is to set zero defects as the goal for every activity, including the invisible ones. Open the scope of your continuous improvement to everything. A dollar here is equal to a dollar there.

Here is one more thing about this topic.

A key advantage of the term *zero-based thinking* (Milliken 2017) is the word "zero," because zero is a symbol that can be understood by anyone, in any culture, and in any language. So, it is a great concept because everyone can align toward this concept of zero with a common understanding.

Zero is another type of standard. Without such a standard, there is a tendency to pick and choose what areas will be looked at for improvement and, at the same, implicitly which activities will be ignored.

I will be talking about our responsibility to ensure there is zero discrepancy in between the meanings we exchange. The standard for this is zero ambiguity.

SAM YANKELEVITCH

By the way, zero helps to set a direction. Ladies and gentlemen, it does not mean eliminate everything immediately, but it does drive everyone to scrutinize whether an activity is necessary, what waste it contains, and how it can create waste elsewhere.

Since some of you like to hear Japanese terms, you may be aware of the word *kaizen* and associate it with continuous improvement. But a word we seldom encounter in our quality and continuous improvement journeys is *Haijo* (Nakamuro 2017).

Haijo is a term that refers to keeping an open mind and looking at every activity that must happen for the customer to be served. It helps get us closer to a holistic approach that does not ignore invisible factors.

Kaizen is good, but combined with Haijo and zero base, it is better because it can help us go deeper toward the real source of the issues and all obstacles we need to improve.

In our case, it can help us raise the issue of miscommunication as a strong source of problems in a way no one can oppose. It is a mindset that allows us to see invisible things.

Because of time I have to continue with the next topic, so if you want you can ask about zero later. Thanks.

Session 4

Heightened Interdependence

FOR MANY OF US, ESPECIALLY if we are programmed by Western culture, our social upbringing has been individualistic in nature, and habituated patterns of thinking and acting keep us believing in our individual power; it's the illusion of independence.

Therefore, to counter such engrained patterns, we must keep reminding ourselves of our interdependence.

We are interdependent. Very interdependent. Extremely interdependent.

Accepting and understanding our interdependence lies at the root of solving many of our self-created and reoccurring problems.

Let me illustrate with a dictionary definition. To depend comes from the Latin roots de- *down* and pendere- *to hang on* (or *to hang upon*), which denotes the reliance on something (Online Etymology Dictionary 2018).

From this root we can define:

To be "independent" means the reliance on yourself.

To be "dependent" means reliance on someone or something.

To be "interdependent" means to be dependent on each other. It's about a mutual relationship where there is benefit to all interdependent parties. *Mutual* makes all the difference.

In the current context of business, the illusion of independence can cause unwanted costs in your organization. This illusion also causes a disconnect with the customer.

Interdependence of people

As much as we would like to believe our individualistic thoughts, the reality is that in business everything we do requires more than just ourselves.

Gone are the days when craftsmen thought of an idea, designed it, selected the materials, and handcrafted their own inventions with self-made tools.

Things changed with the Industrial Revolution, when the progression from idea to design, to tooling and manufacturing, to assembly, packaging, and delivery began to happen across multiple sites. Players began to specialize in any of the steps needed to satisfy a customer, but, unfortunately, they did not specialize in improving their communication skills.

Change may have come too quickly for our minds to catch up and understand that we cannot get things done by ourselves. With the division of steps in a process came the increased need to coordinate with others, to make sure everyone is doing what they need to do, when it needs to be done, and how it needs to be done, along with how each role affects the other.

Besides our biased beliefs of our independence, the charts and maps we have adopted continue to act as barriers to seeing other factors that affect our results. They could be interpreted as confirmation of the illusion we have that we are independent.

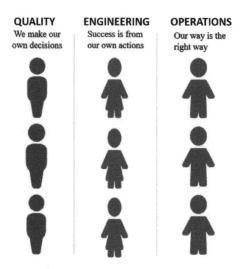

The illusion of independent functions is a key contributor to organizational miscommunication that triggers unwanted costs. The customer is not taken into consideration when independent teams don't coordinate or align.

For example, typical organizational charts that show the standard vertical flow from top to bottom seldom depict the actual flow of information and activities required to satisfy a customer.

Even though it takes requests, instructions, and establishing and keeping commitments horizontally and diagonally across the vertical lines and outside the organization to deliver what the customer wants, there is little to show how every area depends on the other to satisfy the end customer.

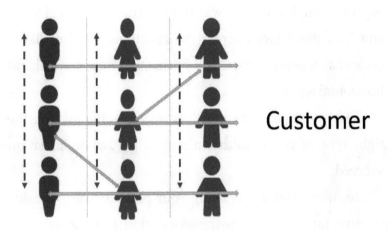

Information, requests, and expectations need to also flow horizontally and diagonally to ensure value is being added from the perspective of the customer.

This flow and exchange of information, both vertical and horizontal, is typically not explicitly expressed by an organizational chart, which leads to unclear and ambiguous interactions.

Here's something to think about when you look at your organization chart. Many of my clients have used the word *silo* to talk about vertical hierarchies that don't talk to other functions. I prefer to see things a bit differently, because the silos are not a bad thing in and of themselves.

Each function does have the technical expertise in their own domain, and that expertise is indispensable to the organization. So, a better way is when there is vertical focus and horizontal focus across the functions, kind of like a cycle that repeats vertical and horizontal, then vertical and horizontal again.

This cycling back and forth is what is going to drive the right type of communication and help your organization succeed.

So, when you are drawing your process maps or value streams for the physical transformation process steps for materials and components, don't leave out the required mapping to drive effective interactions between all the stakeholders.

The goal at every intersection between vertical and horizontal has to align with the customer, and value has to be added when people interact in that intersection.

Coordination without alignment?

Surely, we have to be able to coordinate activities between all interdependent parties.

Without adequate coordination, all parties will ultimately be affected by the waste that takes place in any step of the process. Without alignment, however, interdependent players might be contributing to waste in critical value chains, especially if they are moving in distinctly separate directions.

If we continue to live in denial of our interdependence, cause and effect will definitely have an uncontrolled impact on our interactions – and our results.

This next slide can help you understand what each concept means in the context of interdependence.

Here is my distinction between the two concepts:

While **coordination** refers to the organization of different elements taking part in executing tasks in a way that enables each part to work together effectively, **alignment** refers to the arrangement of elements moving in a joint, common direction toward a defined and accepted goal.

Both concepts, alignment and coordination, create a sense of interrelatedness, but at the same time they point out the uniqueness of each player, recognizing each one's specific capabilities and expertise.

It is through respect of our mutual uniqueness and accepting mutual interdependence that team players can move in one common direction.

While internal teams may be coordinating their activities adequately, each separate site may be working on different priorities, either because their local strategic goals are different or because of scheduling circumstances that drive priorities a certain way.

Also, each participating site may be part of a different legal entity, perhaps with conflicting priorities. The strategic direction of each separate entity will influence its individual priorities.

Too many strategies are designed based on the illusion of independence. This generates a lot of waste because of misaligned tasks. It is often the reason for poor quality, late deliveries, and premium costs.

Networks of teams

If supply chains are responsible for delivering a product or service to a customer, what are these chains actually made of?

In my mind, the word "chain" brings up a metallic sense – maybe even a chain that is used to keep something from moving. Two synonyms of *chain* are shackle and restraint.

Please try to use a better word so it matches the intent of the gemba we are talking about and because humans are at the core of these interlinked processes.

To be more specific, it is teams made up of humans with unique and specific roles that need to work in a coordinated way to achieve a defined goal. In the case of a manufacturing environment, each function required to produce the end product is organized as a team responsible to execute specific tasks and activities.

For each step of the process in a supply chain, there might be different teams interacting with each other, which can mean an exchange of information between people from the same function, for example, engineers with engineers, or engineers with marketing personnel.

In numerous supply chains where personnel are well trained to execute and perform their tasks, most of them are highly skilled in their own technical area – that is, experts in their processes – who possess the know-how to ensure physical processes and procedures are followed.

Unfortunately, in these very same chains I continue to encounter waste in the form of scrap, rework, or premium transportation costs where the teams have attributed the source to some type of miscommunication.

As it turns out, while most team members are highly skilled for dealing with technical tasks, they are not very skilled in effectively interacting with others. Their expertise and focus are elsewhere, mostly on technical skills.

With the limited amount of time available to execute and get things done, we tend to tackle those tasks that are tangible and visible, thus neglecting and ignoring other more invisible tasks. As a result, little attention is paid to factors that might be robbing time – the most precious and irreplaceable resource.

Therefore, any potential contributing cause for loss of time needs to be examined. If miscommunication fits into this category, then it needs to be included, as should any other waste that needs scrutiny.

I hope to have heightened your awareness about the reality of our interdependence.

If there are some questions now, I would like to hear them.

Attendee 15: *Hello Mr. Onata-San, I enjoyed the redefinition of coordination and alignment. It is clear alignment is about moving in the same direction, but I've seen where separate teams are not following the same timelines, such as in projects. What is missing? What can be improved to really be effective with interdependence?*

Mr. Onata: Oh yes, good point. The time factor in the case of projects is very critical. The term I like is *synchronization,* because *synchro* is associated with time. From the Greeks, *syn* is together and *chronos* is time.

The trio you can adopt is synchronization, coordination, and alignment.

If a timeline is imposed without understanding or with no mutual agreement, there can be synchronization problems. Timelines, when not clearly explained, can create confusion, and then not everyone will be on the same page.

You ask what can be improved? I would like to address your question through the concept of respect. I will bring this concept into the presentation again later as well.

For now, it makes sense to accept that we are interdependent. This does not mean we all have to think alike or that we have to change our ways. But it does bring the need to acknowledge and respect the different needs and wants of each partner.

But to answer the young lady's question, along with respect we need to act with transparency. Transparency can be a guide to a common understanding for everyone to be on the same page.

Transparency helps us see why others are acting the way they do, so we can avoid assuming that they just randomly want to do things differently.

Transparency can help people understand where their partners are, what circumstances they are working in, and, more importantly, why they are expecting something to be done in a specific time.

Usually there is an end customer tied to a timeline, so this should always be the reason why everyone respects a timeline.

These are very tough things for many organizations. This presentation is about raising the awareness and laying the groundwork – maybe planting a seed that will bring improvement.

And we better move in that direction, before we are all replaced by robots.

Chronos is reminding me that it's about time. Ready for a quick break? I'll see you in 10 minutes.

Interactions: the core of getting things done

Now we have to discuss how it is that things get done. Physical things.

Things don't become tangible and concrete on their own.

In business, things start out as ideas, which then evolve into products and services that are perceived as valuable to customers. This process from idea to concreteness requires the coordination of multiple activities, whereby in an interdependent world those activities are generated through the interactions of one or more persons.

Human interactions are at the core of getting things done, and at the core of an interaction is the process of communication.

During an interaction, an exchange is happening; it could be a transfer of an idea, knowledge, requests, or instructions intended to ultimately create physical transformation, ending with a tangible outcome. While I use the words *concrete, physical,* or *tangible,* it's important to clarify that I do not wish to exclude services or such things as information or software, which also result from exchanges between two or more people or systems.

Concrete is also meant to be understood as something of value, something that will solve a problem, bring benefit, or even simply create a positive emotion, by filling a need. The value is, of course, as perceived by the customer.

So, physical activities and tasks are powered by interactions. Lean and other continuous improvement systems help us focus on seeing how each activity adds value and where there may be waste that we can reduce or remove. At the same time, this means avoiding defects.

But how often do we look at the human interaction that originated and triggered the physical activity?

Do we have a way to determine if the interaction itself is adding value?

What wastes might be present in the process of the interaction itself?

Can an interaction trigger waste in the physical realm?

Did the meanings match the first time?

Do you have a standard for what a quality interaction is?

The Process

Many of you will have seen some version of a mechanical model of communication, which as I said lies at the heart of any interaction. The sender sends a message and the receiver interprets the message.

This is a simplified model that we will have to examine more deeply, so we can use it in a business setting, where the ultimate purpose is to create value for the customer. Remember, we interact to create something tangible.

Let's talk about the message as an instruction that is being sent to another person, or by one system to another, in the case of IT systems. Inside this message, there is a meaning that reflects the core concept or idea of whatever the instruction is supposed to generate physically.

So, the receiver is interpreting the meaning that the sender transmitted. If the interpretation of the meaning by the receiver is 100% the same as the intended meaning of the sender, bthen we have a value-added interaction.

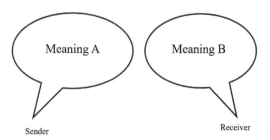

Words don't have meanings, people do. A message being sent contains meaning A, based on the context and understanding of the sender. The receiver will understand the meaning B, based on his or her understanding and context.

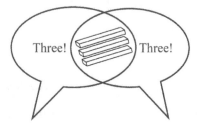

The sender on the left requested three sticks, and the receiver on the right has the same understanding.

The meanings match. So, insofar as the actual activity of interacting, we can say we have an effective interaction.

Here's the important part. When meanings don't match, we say we have a bad interaction, or a nonconformance. But the problem does not stop there, because we also said the interaction was intended to create physical value. Therefore, we can label a bad interaction a *misunderstanding*.

Plus, we know that taking action based on a misunderstanding carries a higher risk that the physical execution will have problems, and this can contribute to negative results.

Here are three things about communication:

1. Communication is invisible.
2. Communication is a process.
3. Communication precedes action.

No. 3 states: Communication precedes action. Now we can better see how we trigger bad actions – bad physical processes – just because we lack a clear understanding of what has to be done.

Value-added interactions

Every time we interact with someone, we have to consider that the intended meaning might not match the interpreted meaning.

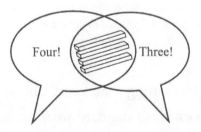

In a more complex situation, the sender on the left is requesting four sticks, but the receiver on the left is understanding three sticks, which is a noncon-formance in the process of communication. The outcome of this interaction can yield a bad physical outcome, e.g., a defect.

The goal is to ensure a value-added interaction, meaning that there is a common understanding between the sender and the receiver. I like the term *unambiguous* because it comes from the very root of the word meaning. Ambiguous can have more than one meaning; unambiguous is the opposite, and that's what we want – one shared common meaning that is understood the same way by everyone.

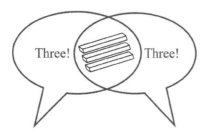

The goal is ambiguity = 0
Zero is the standard

The word ambiguous means something can have more than one meaning. It can drive confusion because things can be understood in many ways. If no standard exists, everyone will proceed to act the way they each believe is the right way.

We are in fact setting a standard. This is similar to the work we do to establish standard work on our shop floors. Our goal then should be to ensure those two meanings match 100%, to achieve an unambiguous result of the interaction itself.

What is the problem here?

One of the other key points of communication, that it is invisible, is quite a problem. Because we cannot see the actual meanings being exchanged, we cannot know for sure if they match. We may find out when it's too late and the physical activity that was triggered resulted in problems – physical problems that are being measured and to which a cost can be attached.

I do think that by coming to this conference you are becoming aware of things you may have not have considered before. Awareness is the first step to making the invisible visible.

And how about, "Communication is a process." Perhaps if we map the process, the invisible can become clearer in our minds. A map is a good way to illustrate, to represent things, to model processes.

We started to show a mechanical model of the process of communication, and this can be expanded to show more details of how meanings flow and how meanings are changed or transformed along the way. And maybe as some of you are trained to do a value stream map, we can also begin to visualize where value can be negatively affected.

Where can we have waste? Where can we have defects in our interactions? I will talk more about mapping later, when we talk about solutions. Before that, however, the model needs a small change, one that can make a big difference.

The human model

If you were paying attention when I referred to this model of communication, I called it the "mechanical model," which doesn't really represent reality, considering that the interactions I have discussed are those between people. So, I would like to change the model a bit from sender and receiver, to supplier and customer.

And please remember that teams and organizations don't talk to each other. Humans do.

This makes it a human process. And by recognizing this, we cannot avoid our responsibility to ensure that every interaction is one where meanings match. It is our duty to try to get the meaning right the first time, and if this does not happen immediately, we must strive to get there.

This means there will be a give and take, a feedback loop between the customer and the supplier, where the customer becomes the supplier and the supplier becomes the customer, alternating until the meaning being conveyed matches. In other words, this goes on until an unambiguous standard is reached.

Take note that this model makes things more interesting because the attention we pay when dealing with our customer is typically of better quality. We tend to take the time to really understand the expectations of our customer; we try harder to reach clarity and 100% understanding of what is going to satisfy them.

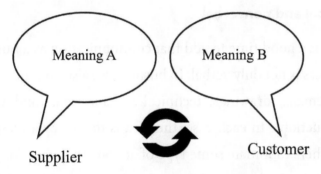

When we respect and care, a relationship forms between a customer and a supplier of information. The added attention and responsibility can help improve communication and, therefore, physical outcomes.

Communication is happening inside a relationship that requires certain expectations and requests from the customer to be fulfilled by the supplier. Communicating inside a relationship creates a different level of attention and caring, and it leads to an attitude of responsibility and respect.

This new model is of great help in remembering that we are dealing with other humans when we are trying to communicate. If we are initializing the interaction, then we are the supplier and they are our customer.

We want to make sure we are doing everything possible to be understood, to get our message across clearly, so others can be successful in their tasks.

Verbal and nonverbal

This is a good time to add that communication as a human process is not only verbal. In business we also communicate via emails, drawings, technical specifications, and work instructions. In each case, the idea is to convey a message to others to initiate some type of action. Therefore, keep in mind that our responsibility to be clear also applies in these cases.

It is time for some more questions or a discussion, and then we will part for a short lunch break.

Attendee 7: *Mr. Onata, since you mentioned mapping, what can we change, or learn, when we are doing our value stream maps?*

Mr. Onata: Thank you for that question. Here is a quick story that may help illustrate. Last year I visited a chemical company, and it had a wall-to-wall value stream map prepared by the continuous improvement team. They had placed many sticky notes to identify opportunities or show where further information was needed.

The interesting thing is that they had numerous sticky notes on the raw materials and the chemical processing streams, as well as a few sticky notes on the signals coming from their customers.

Therefore, I asked what those sticky notes meant – the ones from the customer signals – and the reply was: "The signal is sometimes not clear," "We get multiple signals for the same demand," "Their IT system does not talk to our IT system," and "Often because of these problems, our production planning is chaotic, and our plants have to stop and restart other orders."

So, I asked, "Is your continuous improvement team working with your customer to fix this, so their signal is clear and does not trigger any waste in your physical processes?"

"Nope!" was the answer. The focus of the continuous improvement team was exclusively on the physical transformation processes.

Does this make sense? No attention was being paid to the stream that was triggering physical waste. So, we have to pay equal attention to the first stream and all the signals between our internal processes as well.

Is every signal on your value stream map 100% clear? Are you applying your quality and continuous improvement to the signals that you map on your value streams?

Attendee 12: *Dear sir, you did say the model you have shown us is summarized. If we really want to pay attention to every step in a communication process, and at the same time maybe use that in a value stream map, what would you say are the other steps? This would also help shine a light on those steps, right?*

Mr. Onata: For sure, there are several steps, and I will share with you my interpretation, based on work from my seminars. Let me use this virtual board to write the steps.

I would like to start with the first step, the thought or idea in the mind of one person. Step 1: idea.

Because we are in a business context, there is an expectation of a task to be performed by someone, in order to fill a customer expectation.

Here I'd like to make an interim step where the idea is transformed into a request, an instruction, or just a piece of information needed by the other person. So, let's call that step 2: transforming the idea into a request.

In step 3 the person with the request has to choose the medium, the way he or she will send the message to the other person. This is a key point, because it makes you consider the best way to ensure nothing from the meaning will be lost, depending on who will be receiving the message.

For example, keep in mind that emails and text messages are excellent ways to create confusion and that these are great media to misinterpret the original intended meaning of a communication – especially if the people interacting don't know each other well enough.

Then, in step 4, the person chooses the words, symbols, and pictures that can assure the message is understood; that is, they craft the message. Then, in step 5, they send the message.

The next step is something I learned from my seminars. It's a choice the other person has to make, and it's about listening. Let's call step 6 availability.

If we are very busy, we may not be available to listen, or maybe the message is so complicated or overwhelming that it creates a natural barrier and drives us to choose to pay attention to something else. Not being available to listen represents a breakdown in the communication process.

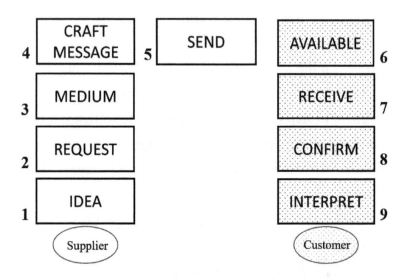

This is an expanded version of steps in the communication process. Stop and think what might disrupt the process at each step for the supplier? For the customer?

Multitasking for example often creates a problem of availability to listen.

Step 7, receive, is about receiving the request. I think of this like a mechanical process, and Step 8, confirm, involves immediately acknowledging to the supplier of the message that it was received. Acknowledging that we have listened, deliberately, with full commitment to understand, is also part of respect, because we are letting the other person know we received the message, we are processing the message.

Acknowledging is also what I think kicks off the intention to dialogue later, as it shows interest and engagement in an interdependent process.

Then, in step 9: interpret, the receiving person understands and makes sense of the message.

This interpretation is dependent on the context, which is part of the message, but the words will also be interpreted based on the context with which the receiver associates the words. There is a combination of possible contexts here.

Interpretation is where a lot of variation is possible. There are many factors affecting this step, and we need to be highly aware of them. Therefore, as a measure to reduce variation, we can initiate a feedback loop.

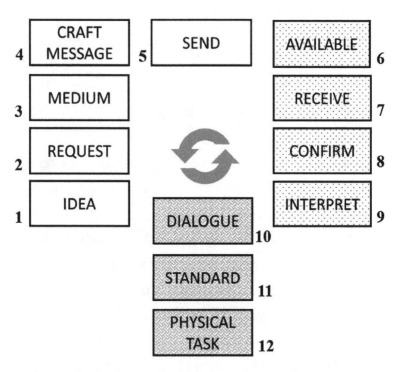

After a cycle of exchanges of meanings occur between the customer and the supplier, an agreement can be obtained about fulfilling the intent of a request or an expectation. Each party will act based on an unambiguous standard.

I like the word *dialogue*, instead of *feedback*, so dialogue is step 10.

In contrast, I think monologue is what happens until we dialogue; it's a one-way independent action. The dialogue is interdependent, it is meant to clarify and bring to the surface our interpretations, preferably in the form of a question. Remember, when we ask a question, it prompts the other person to engage to understand.

Dialogue is the engine that drives the rotation cycle between supplier and customer in a continuous exchange of meanings, where a customer becomes a supplier and a supplier becomes a customer, until an agreement can be established. The agreement is step 11, and I call this an *unambiguous standard*, a standard that points back to the word "common," as in common understanding, with *common* serving as the root of the word communication.

Then, when communication really happens, we can move with less risk to the last step, which is physical action. It is less risky because we have a standard way to clearly understand what tasks and activities need to be done. Not having this agreement, everyone might do something different than expected, with potential for physical waste.

Step 12 is physical action, the tasks that transform tangible things.

Please note that waste, or non-value-added activity, can therefore happen in any of these steps, or perhaps in between any of the steps.

So, this is one way to map this invisible process and visualize it, and bring it to the surface so we can walk it.

I see there is someone with a pressing question, please go ahead.

Attendee 13: *Mr. Onata, isn't physical action separate from the communication process? Why do you include it as step 12?*

Mr. Onata: Yes, that is a great question. I have a bit of a philosophical reply, and perhaps a bit scientific.

To address your question, we treat many things separately. As humans we love to label things so our brains can make sense of the world. In this case, we have chosen to label the physical things as actions and activities. These are tangible things.

But invisible things, which we pay less attention to, we omit from this label.

In some circles, we would be labeling these invisible things as "soft." This is a very bad label, as there's nothing *soft* about communication and interactions, especially if they have hard influence on the physical activities.

Let's imagine an avocado tree. When I look at it, I see the fruits, the leaves, and the trunk, and I know there are roots under the ground. What I also know is that at one point in time there was a seed. And that seed is a part of this tree, and it is still contained inside the fruits.

The seed is hidden under the earth, but it created the physical trunk and leaves, by interacting in an interdependent way with the soil, the water and the sun.

In that case the seed is a part of the process, just like communication is often the seed of physical activities.

A bad seed might result in a bad tree, and bear bad fruit Communication "pre-seeds" action. It is the seed of physical action.

I look at the physical action as the tree and the seed as the communication, all as one, not separate.

Well, perhaps this is also a bit scientific.

Now I am very hungry. Maybe there will be some avocado on the menu. Will you join me for lunch?

Session 6

The Dicula Triangle

IN THIS SESSION I WOULD like to illustrate three factors that you may find in your organizations that can be causes of variation.

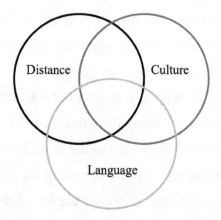

The Dicula Triangle represents three types of sources of variation that exist in organizations.

Because each of these factors can be affected by the other, the situation that results is somewhat dynamic and complex, but we have to remind ourselves that they exist.

I know some of you like to have an easy way to remember a concept, so with your permission, may we call this the "Dicula Triangle"? DI for distance, CU for culture, and LA for language.

Let's dissect the Dicula Triangle in this slide.

Culture is not a simple topic; it's somewhat fuzzy and abstract. Maybe we can also add this to the list of invisible factors.

Think of culture as the programming we have received from the different groups we belong to. So, national culture is related to the overall country culture you were born into and specific to the region of that country. There are also cultural differences between engineers and controllers, and also quality and logistics, for example.

Be careful of generalizing a country's culture. It's like saying all Americans think the same and behave the same way, or that people in India are all the same. But the southern and northern regions of these countries are quite different, and the norms of behavior in each are also different.

There are also generations, immigrations, and education that will create differences within the same nationality.

Here is a magic word that can help you avoid generalizing. It is the word *some*. *Some* Japanese are nice, *some* Americans are nice, and so on.

Culture is also associated with the organizations for which we work. When the processes and procedures that people follow drive successful outcomes, these ways to work are adopted as the "right" ways to work and become the norm, therefore helping to create a culture.

Culture and behavior are tied, just like systemic cause and effect. Culture drives behavior, and behavior drives culture.

If we have been brought up a specific way, it will drive us to behave a certain way, and often this happens subconsciously. We don't realize this programming causes us to act a certain way.

Then when we have to work with people from another culture, and their behavior seems odd, we ask, "Why do they act so weird?"

Because I have lived so many years outside of Japan, I'm seeing things from the outside. I can identify the invisible programming of my fellow Japanese, whereas they are acting automatically without noticing how their Japanese traditions are impacting their relationships with other non-Japanese people.

This may not be a problem if you are on vacation and something odd happens, then you laugh and learn. But if the behaviors, or reactions, affect the work you are supposed to be doing together, then there can be a cost impact associated with a cultural misunderstanding.

A few years ago, I flew to Japan with one of my American clients to visit a supplier of special electronic components. This was the first visit to the Japanese company.

You may already know about bowing respectfully to say hello and to introduce each other – and this went about quite smoothly.

Then we sat down, and the head person from the Japanese company began to show a presentation about the origins, the company founders, and their humble beginnings. This presentation went on for about 30-40 minutes, and my client was continuously looking at his watch. I could sense that he was anxious to get on with the business topics. A translator was also present.

When the presentation ended, after a short silent pause, my client started talking about why he was in Japan, the project his company was working on, and the importance of the component he was there to negotiate.

I did not intervene, as I was only a guest, consulting with no real rank in the American company. And surely enough,

I knew quite well what was probably going on in the minds of the Japanese.

The translator came back with a question to my client about where he was born, if he liked baseball, and if he had children, to which he responded: "I will get to that after I present our requirements and specs."

Then my client opened his laptop and requested access to the projector, and showed the components and drawings on the screen, along with a critical timeline of the project and the importance of the component.

By now, the Japanese team looked annoyed.

I remember Mr. Nakamura, the head person at the conference table, turned to the translator with a few short words, which the translator repeated back to my client: "Dear Mr. James, we will stop our meeting now and go for dinner at 7 p.m. See you tonight."

That was the end of the meeting. My client had not advanced one millimeter insofar as the business terms and possibilities to order the component from this company. In his head, his afternoon had been a waste of time. Before we left the conference room, he wrote down some key points he was planning to ask during dinner, to advance a bit on his questions.

As he mentioned the questions to me, I told him to put them away and not bring up the business topic during dinner.

Sorry, I need to make this story short, but the details until now were important for you to grasp how the different views affected their business.

First of all, dinner worked out very well because we all drank sake and beer, sake and beer, and more sake and beer. No problems at dinner – everyone got to know each other a bit better.

The next day, however, my client requested an estimate of the lead time to design, develop, and produce the component, to which the Japanese manager replied, "18 weeks." My American client replied in a slightly arrogant tone, "Well, that cannot be. We need it in six weeks. You must be able to get it done in six weeks. This is a $20 million buy we will be making."

Then, the Japanese manager folded his notebook and said in perfect English, "Dear Mr. James, thank you for coming to Japan and visiting us. He got up, his staff got up, and the meeting was over."

No pricing. No lead time. No component. And now for my client, the project was at risk.

What happened? Did culture influence the results of this interaction?

Time is money. This is the value that got in the way, because for each it had a different meaning.

My client was all about getting things done quickly. For him, the pleasantries of getting to know each other were not important. Learning about the Japanese company's origins was not important.

Surely, he thought, $20 million should get anyone's attention. He had been programmed by both his upbringing and the corporate culture, and he behaved according to that programming.

On the other hand, the Japanese team needed to establish with *whom* they were going to enter into a business relationship. And for the Japanese, this can be quite complex, perhaps more related to the human, moral, and ethical components that could help establish a bond of trust. They will even be curious about everyone's place in the hierarchy of society.

Now, this group of Japanese businessmen also has a concept about time and money. They prefer to invest time upfront, to understand the complete scope of the business and their partner's expectations, before launching a project.

My Japanese dad used to say: "Time brings money. Invest time in the relationship at the beginning, the money will come out at the end."

Culture is not just a fuzzy, abstract thing the HR team has to deal with. It's a reality that affects many interactions – the same interactions that trigger tangible results.

And this is only one side of the Dicula Triangle.

Let's discuss the second factor in this diagram: language.

We don't only encounter people who speak other languages when we transact business across the globe. Immigration waves have spread people from many countries into businesses, so we may have in our own organization people whose native tongue is not English.

Speaking the language of the person you need to interact with allows you to get closer to a shared understanding.

I mention this, but trying to stay in the scope of business for this conference, in most Western settings, the English language is the one chosen for interactions. It becomes a standard, and once this is agreed to by the interdependent teams, then language ceases to be a problem. Right? Well, not exactly.

In my experience, I have seen many misunderstandings created between people who were speaking English to each other. We cannot assume everyone speaks it at the same level. Someone educated in England, the United States, or Canada will tend to have a higher level of English than someone who, for example, learned it in high school in France.

This can potentially lead to different meanings, even when the same language is being spoken. So, we can say we have variation within the same language, and matching the meanings between two or more people might prove to be a bit challenging.

When I first came to this country, my boss once said, "Even if you have to burn the midnight oil, I need you to get this done. Jump through hoops if you have to!" In my mind I was thinking about a lot of physical action and creating a fire hazard with some oil.

My colleague translated for me, and it made it clear that we had to work until the job was done. No need to burn any oil or define the specification for the oil to be burned.

When I talk about language, I also add acronyms, because in almost every business these abbreviated forms of speech are used. It's funny, maybe the abbreviations are intended to save time, but in reality, time is not saved, as often these create more problems because not everyone knows what they mean.

Acronyms may represent a combination of corporate culture and language and can benefit those who belong. For everyone else, they are a potential source of misunderstandings and, in any case, the idea of saving time goes away once one has to explain what the abbreviation means. If not explained, they can cause misunderstandings that lead to delays, defects, and unwanted costs.

Let's revisit the circles.

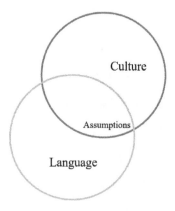

While it's inherently human to make assumptions, we should be aware when we make them. When multiple languages meet diverse cultures, assumptions are likely to happen. The problem is not in the making; it's in acting on them that can cause unwanted costs.

At the intersection of language and culture is the word "assumptions." One definition for assumptions, found in the dictionary, says: "A thing that is accepted as true or as certain to happen, without proof" (Oxford Dictionaries 2018).

Each person in an interaction assumes something. One assumes she is understood, the other assumes he is understood. But, in reality, the meaning being exchanged does not match.

This is very typical for interactions between people from different cultures, because even with a translation, there is a problem related to context. Each word we learn has a context attached to it so we can understand the meaning. Therefore, different cultures have developed in different contexts, and the meanings of words can be quite different.

Many people come to my conferences and pick up on an idea here and there, but during the breaks, one of the most-asked questions or comments has to do with the idea of having to slow down in order to move fast.

This is a difficult thing to do because we are always rushing, thinking that everything we do has to be done quickly. This is a bad habit.

When interacting with others, especially for the first time when we don't know the other person's way of understanding, if we don't slow down, chances are we will commit the mistake of giving life to assumptions.

The person originating the message can make the assumption that he or she is understood.

The person interpreting the message can make the assumption that he or she understood.

One way we can visualize an assumption is as a gap that occurs between an intended meaning and the interpreted meaning.

Until this point, the waste that has happened is the time and energy spent during that interaction, because no value has been added. The plot thickens, however, and things can get worse.

When either or both parties proceed to act based on their own assumptions is when the outcomes of their actions must be watched carefully, because chances are there will be trouble.

Remember this: what is worse than making an assumption?

Acting on one, because this is when things can get costly.

We believe we understand, we think we know the truth, and then we act on it. This is a close cousin of jumping to conclusions. Both of these human habits happen mostly because we go too fast and don't slow down to clarify and remove ambiguity.

Acting based on assumptions is like working without a standard or common meaning. Each person works differently, and this is a type of variation that creates opportunities for poor quality or delivery at a physical level.

In summary, if we choose not to slow down during an interaction, the risk of a bad physical outcome increases.

Does anyone have questions about this?

Attendee 18: *Mr. Onata, what can you add about making assumptions about people? It seems like we tend to make assumptions with some people more often than with others?*

Mr. Onata: Well, I can share an example of a typical mistake team members make in global situations. It turns out that when we see people who look like us, we believe they also think like us and understand things the same way we do. Of course, this is not always true.

As humans, we have an internal mechanism that alerts us to differences, and this same mechanism can help stop our habit of going too fast during an interaction. This built-in alert can help us avoid problems when it notices differences.

What I'm saying is that especially when people look similar to us, we need to make a special effort to slow down until we can be more confident that our message is being properly understood. We need to catch ourselves doing this.

One more question about this topic?

Attendee 19: *Can we adapt any of our lean methodologies to make assumptions visible?*

Mr. Onata: Sure, I can think of a way, and it's up to you if you can accept to work with it. Do you remember 5S? The 5Ss are sort, set in order, shine, standardize, and sustain. When we sort things out in any process, we are looking to select those things that add value and remove those that do not.

Assumptions are temporary outcomes of a communication process that typically add no value. So why not become very aware during an interaction about the possibility of assumptions? Then you can sort these out and remove them.

How do you remove them? You can do this by asking questions and entering into a dialogue to clarify the intended meaning. Assumptions dissolve when they are brought to the surface.

This is like stating your assumptions out loud or broadcasting them.

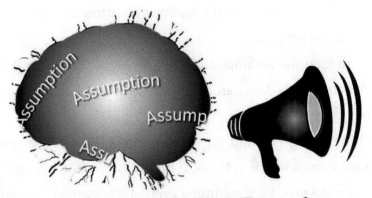

Assume Out Loud

One way to bring invisible assumptions to the surface and make them visible is to make them out loud so others can understand your meaning and context.

This is part of respect for people, sharing why you think this or that, or what your understanding is of something, so the other can grasp your true meaning. It is the proof needed to dissolve the assumption. Then it is impossible to act on an assumption.

You can also visualize the gap between the intended meaning and the interpreted meaning, and set out to close that gap through dialogue and root cause analysis.

There is a notable example I encountered when doing some business in Mexico. The word for "morning" in Mexico is "mañana," translated as "tomorrow." So, you would expect that when someone says "tomorrow" it means the day after today. In too many situations, however, it means "this will eventually get done."

I made the assumption that it would be done the day after today. My Mexican colleagues assumed I understood that it would *eventually* get done.

We can go on and on with examples. Will you please share some with me at the next break?

By the way, I am assuming everyone present is human? Please raise your hand if you are not.

Making assumptions is a human thing; we just have to catch ourselves in the act and bring them to the surface.

Let's revisit the circles and talk about distance.

Ladies and gentlemen, we pay little attention to distance, and I think out of the three factors, it is the one that may cause the most trouble.

Distance is not only physical distance, but also distance created by a feeling. For example, have you ever considered "us and them"? Let me play a little game with you today.

Please close your eyes. Thank you.

Now, imagine you are *here*.

Now, still with your eyes closed, imagine you are *over there*. Thank you.

Now think of *those guys over there*.

And think of *us over here*.

OK. You can open your eyes now. Did some of you *feel* movement? When I do this, I can feel the separation between *here* and *there* – between *us* and *them*.

What does this have to do with distance and communication?

The same way we mentally separate here and there, we tend to feel differently about us and them. In fact, in my seminars when we are discussing the topic, participants have referred to other people as "those guys," accompanied usually by a judgement or critique about how "those guys" behave or the problem with "those guys."

This mental separation is a barrier in itself because communication is a human process, and we have to care about getting it right. This is the same way we would be dealing with our customer.

Therefore, we should stay aware that "those guys" are our customers for information and instructions, and it is our job to communicate clearly.

I also want to mention that distance creates problems in cross-functional situations even inside the same organization. It's really an imaginary line that is made up between departments and the illusion of space separates teams of people who must interact to satisfy a customer.

Our success is interdependent.

Distance is also measured in time zones, and when we are separated by more than six time zones, it's tough to interact effectively. When some players are starting their day, others might be finishing their day, and there is an inherent problem of availability.

Interactions that require clarification or feedback from someone in another time zone will suffer delays; therefore, the tasks and activities that the interaction is intended to trigger will also have to wait.

For those of you who are still worried about the seven wastes, waiting is one of them, right?

While waiting can be wasteful, coordination and synchronization with others also has to happen. Sometimes we have to wait to make sure everyone is on the same page.

So, we can say that time zones can be a contributing source of waste in the communication process.

Let's get back to our drawing with the three circles, the Dicula Triangle.

In this slide I am adding some results or effects at the intersection of each of these factors, trying to further illustrate how these are relevant to our topic. These are not the only possible effects, but they do reflect what I have seen over the years in my walks.

I already mentioned how when we have people from different cultures, the words exchanged can mean different things to different people. And if we are not paying attention, we could assume we understand the other person.

In the intersection of these two circles, culture and language, I have written assumptions.

Now, let's merge the distance circle with the other two circles.

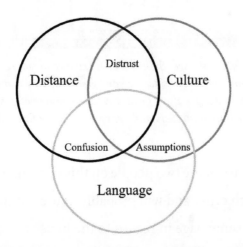

Confusion and distrust are two other factors that influence communication in organizations and originate in the Dicula Triangle.

At the intersection of distance and language I noted *confusion*, because interactions between people who are physically distant are negatively influenced when words are not accompanied by body language.

When we're sitting across from someone, we have a human ability through hand gestures, facial movements, and other body signals, to help clarify the intended meaning.

In face-to-face exchanges there is a better chance to reduce ambiguity because communication is aided by hand gestures, facial expressions, and other nonverbal cues. It's also a great way to establish relationships that can help reduce misunderstandings even when not face to face.

In the case of the two people on this slide, they are sitting close to each other and will probably figure out that they are not on the same page in regard to the house to be built.

To further compound the problem, I mentioned that words drive meaning through the specific context of the interaction. Therefore, consider that when we interact with someone who is sitting on the dark side of the globe, we may not grasp that they may associate a different context and meaning to the same word.

Think of the word *confusion* as it relates to meanings. It carries a lot of uncertainty, possibly leading to unstable processes.

The other intersection is distance and culture. And I wrote *distrust* in there.

Trust can be defined in many ways: This is a dictionary definition: "firm belief in the reliability, truth, ability, or strength of someone or something" (Oxford Dictionaries 2018).

It is a belief, a feeling.

And distance can make it difficult to believe in something that is remote, separated by many miles, so we have a tough time *feeling* about it. And because trust is key to establishing adequate relationships for interactions to be effective, this is something to consider.

In other words, the lack of trust can create a barrier – an obstacle to the flow of communication.

The three circles also intersect, and this central intersection I will simply refer to as *variation*.

Please remember the statement from Dr. W. Edwards Deming that I mentioned earlier: "Uncontrolled variation is the enemy of quality."

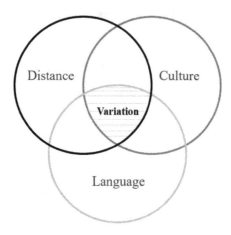

Variation in your physical processes might be the result of the uncontrolled variation inherent to the Dicula Triangle.

These three factors, ladies and gentlemen, are contributing sources of variation in our physical processes. We cannot seek to establish some kind of control or really improve our processes without taking note and responsibility for the impact these hidden, overlooked factors have on our outcomes.

Please keep this Dicula Triangle in your minds when you are designing, planning, and problem solving.

This has been a long session, and we all need a break. But I will open for at least one more question, and we can deal with other questions after the break. OK?

Attendee 8: *Mr. Onata, thank you for that diagram. My question is more related to things that just now are beginning to make sense to me, from something you said before. Sorry that I am just now bringing this up. It is about the ideas we are so programmed to use when we approach continuous improvement. Like visual management, or the seven wastes. Can this programming get in the way?*

Mr. Onata: Yes sir, it is possible. You asked about visual management, and this is, of course, a very good way to notice what is out of control or not in the standard – or maybe see what is trending in a certain direction. So, it can help us notice waste, or potential for waste, and we can then take action. The problem I see is that visual management can only highlight things our eyes can observe, and it can deceive us into believing we are covering all the possible angles and all the sources of problems. There is a similar issue with the seven wastes, because these are only the ones that were designated many years ago, when production was more local, and the Dicula Triangle did not have such an impact then. Today, the circumstances are not the same. There are new sources of variation that have crept into our processes, and we cannot just continue with our limited traditional approaches. New approaches are needed in the new gemba.

"Unfortunately, real waste lurks in forms that do not look like waste."

Shigeo Shingo (1987)

By the way, this triangle is also related to the Goryō I discussed with Mr. Boern when I was helping him in Germany. Each of these factors is like a ghost. Please see the picture and remember it. It will help you keep these invisible beings in your awareness when you are looking for the causes of a bad result.

One or more of these Goryō could be contributing to your problems.

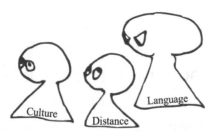

Goryō are vengeful little ghosts that lurk in your processes. You cannot see them, but they are there trying to create chaos and confusion.

So, I hope this has helped clarify your question.

Attendee 8: Yes, thank you!

Mr. Onata: Let's continue with the matter of whose responsibility is this process of communication.

Communication is everyone's job

SO FAR, WE HAVE ALREADY established that interactions between one or more individuals are required to accomplish tasks and activities, and that those interactions have to ensure clarity so the physical outcomes they trigger are successful.

Now that we have brought some invisible things into our awareness, it's quite difficult to forget these exist.

If everyone is now looking out for opportunities to improve each interaction, over time there should be an increase in effective interactions with every opportunity, thus improving the physical process as well.

Here is the problem. Roles and responsibilities greatly influence how team members behave. Organizations are made up of areas and functions where individual players take on a role and wear the hat of a specific function or responsibility.

When participants see themselves as *specialists* and behave based on the unique hat they wear, they will also limit their responsibility. I often hear: "The people from quality are responsible for quality. Human resources for human resources. Finance for financial folks."

This specialization complicates matters even more if our functional filters drive us to separate technical skills from other skills that are popularly labeled as *soft* in many organizations. And it is precisely these other skills that create the connections required for the customer to be served. Whether we pay attention to these skills or not, connections between the different areas are occurring; sometimes they are effective, sometimes they are less effective.

Sometimes they create disasters.

How about we eradicate the term *soft*, and instead label these issues *hard*, because they are hard to see, but also because we may be forced to pay more attention to hard issues due to the hard and costly consequences to which we have seen these factors contribute.

Furthermore, considering that the main focus in getting a job done is mostly on the "technical" aspect, seldom is there consideration about the reality that each function is only part of a whole required to serve the end customer.

All this is part of the illusion that we are independent.

But, it's not up to someone else: all people acquire the responsibility for effective communication, especially if they are initiating an interaction that is going to trigger a physical activity.

Does it make sense then to ensure each role assumes the responsibility for clarity to be achieved with every interaction? The job descriptions and roles might be part of the problem, because they don't always explicitly state how each role contributes to the whole, or how each role must interact with all other roles internally, and with suppliers and customers.

So, we could choose to deliberately complement employees' job descriptions with statements that ensure they pay attention to how they communicate. That is, add to each job description the obligation to effectively interact.

This will provide a better opportunity to improve the quality of interactions between the different areas and functions. In addition, a good level of transparency can be achieved by adding each role's expected contribution to the organization, how that role supports the other roles, and how it all ties together for the benefit of the external customer.

By the way, in business scenarios where interactions are greatly influenced by distance, culture, or different spoken languages, the job description of anyone in these circumstances should carry specific and detailed responsibilities related to the effectiveness of the interactions in which they will be involved.

If these responsibilities are called out, then the organization would also be compelled to change training programs to adjust to this new reality, and upgrade skills and competencies to close the skills gap between the tangible and the invisible.

I want to be clear that it is always better if people can adopt this thinking on their own. In other words, make it their responsibility to ensure quality interactions. But I know this is not always realistic and sometimes, to raise the awareness, we can adjust the job descriptions to support this idea.

So, if we are discussing the quality of our interactions, then these should also be everyone's responsibility.

This is where we can improve on our implicit responsibility: communication is everyone's responsibility.

"EIQI - Every Interaction a Quality Interaction."

Do you know the Japanese term Eiqi? I am just kidding – it's not Japanese at all.

The goal is EIQI – to make every interaction a quality interaction.

And to be clear, we go back to the source of the word communication: common, unambiguous meanings, their meaning is equal to ours, just like a standard.

We must avoid the illusion that communication happened. In every interaction we are looking to have value added, both in the interaction and how it impacts any subsequent physical outcome.

Interactions happen anyway, so we have the choice to continue without attention and leave it up to randomness, or we can become responsible for quality interactions that can lead to tangible quality results.

Responsibility for invisible problem solving

Technical roles such as engineering, IT, supply chain, or finance have methodologies to deal with situations where things don't go according to plan, and for solving certain types of problems as they arise.

So, we may again suffer from labeling and categorizing what is technical and what is not, and then picking and choosing what problems we will or will not be responsible for solving.

Yes, it is our job. All problems must be solved – not only the visible ones.

If the gemba has changed, people must adjust to the new circumstances to ensure the survival and success of the organization.

And, our mindset must change.

As mentioned in previous sessions, problems with human interactions can often be handled in similar ways as physical problems. It's truly a matter of reframing a situation from an abstract, invisible standpoint to making the situation visible and tangible.

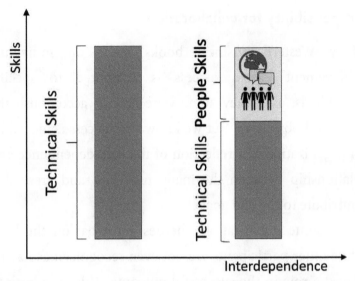

With the increase of interdependence there are additional skills needed to complement our jobs to be successful in the new gemba.

The point here is that most technical roles have been trained to approach and solve problems with certain techniques, methodologies, and tools, and what we need is for people in any functional area to realize that they can adopt the same ways of thinking to solve the so-called soft issues.

This actually strengthens their technical skills with the complementary skills required to accomplish the goals of the job in the new circumstances.

Responsibility for collaboration

Many Western business books focus on individual achievement where success is attributed to specific individuals, as if they alone were able to accomplish the goals and objectives. But we know the success achieved by an organization is a reflection of the interdependence and relationship between the many functions and areas that contribute to the end goals.

In some organizations, heroes get a pat on the back while other participants are not even recognized as having played a role in the successful outcome. This goes back to organizational culture and a traditional way of managing performance on an individual basis.

This points to yet another opportunity for improving the interactions between people in different areas and functions by complementing the performance management system to include *collaboration* as an activity for which every role is responsible.

No collaboration, negative performance review – and no pat on the back.

And now I can respond to some questions.

Attendee 16: *Can you provide an example where we can start taking responsibility? I work with global teams all the time, and it's truly a challenge to ensure everyone is* on the same page. *Personally, I find that when people don't speak English well enough, this is a barrier. What can you recommend?*

Mr. Onata: Dear sir, thank you for the question, and I think your English is much better than mine. So, here is something to think about.

The English language has evolved as the chosen language to transact business for a large portion of the world. If you are a native English speaker, you might take for granted that everyone you interact with will understand what you're saying and grasp the exact meaning of your message. If you are an experienced member of a global supply chain, you know this is not a realistic thought.

. English is not an easy language. Non-native speakers may have learned basic English in school and enter the workforce where they encounter the reality of the language.

Supply chains use specific vocabularies, terms, and technical lingo to support the needs of communicating expectations, requests, and instructions. These will typically be learned by team members over time, considering they are words and language constructs that are used over and over, within the context of something a professional will understand. A known context is a great complement to learning a foreign language.

Many native English speakers are unaware that their accents, the speed of their speech, and their use of idioms make it very challenging for non-native speakers to understand. In such cases, taking responsibility is to become aware of how we are speaking, or how we write email messages.

My American friend told me once that we would just show up and take care of things *on the fly*. In my mind, I was expecting that somehow we would be working that day with flies. I didn't know what he meant. Someone later explained that it means "just do it, without a lot of preparation."

Each team member should take ownership for communicating effectively to ensure each interaction is successful. Slow down the speed of your speech, pronounce the complete words, avoid idioms, and explain them when you do use them.

Please also take care of your acronyms. Every organization seems to make up its own abbreviated versions of concepts or processes. Do not assume the person you are interacting with understands these or will ask what you mean by GGH3.2 or DF-6 rev 45. It is *your* responsibility to explain and clarify. Show respect for people.

Respect is also getting feedback from others, as it is indispensable for knowing what they are understanding.

Take responsibility, slow down, and ask, "Can you please tell me what you understood?" and "What action will you be taking next?" Their success is your success.

Next question?

Attendee 18: *What about the other forms of communication like drawings and work instructions?*

Mr. Onata: Yes, basically it's the same idea.

Taking responsibility also means realizing that when we are putting together work instructions, a technical drawing, or a specification, these are meant to be devices that transmit content that will somehow affect how an activity or task will be done by someone.

We tend to design and write these based on our own context and our own level of understanding.

Therefore, it is our responsibility to consider how the instructions might be perceived or how the drawing might be interpreted by someone with a different worldview who will interpret these in a different context.

It's terrible to still see, in this 21st century, handwritten notes on a document such as a drawing. When we cannot decipher what is written, we must make assumptions and act on assumptions, which can turn out to be costly, and precious time might be wasted.

And let's not forget emails and texts, ladies and gentlemen. These are great opportunities to confuse your partners. When we don't know them, we cannot even guess how they will interpret our writing.

I recommend that if it is the first time you are interacting with someone, if you must initiate the relationship by email, be aware of what you are writing. Send the email, but please also pick up the phone a make a call. Create a relationship with your human voice, mention that you are calling to make sure your message is clear. Ask what the person understood from your email.

This is an opportunity for you to learn how others interpret your messages. Learning is an opportunity to improve.

Again, all this ties back to respect for people, because it shows we care.

Please, some more questions anyone?

Applying Jidoka, the Fishbone, and the 5 Whys to Make the Invisible Visible

ATTENDEE 9: *CAN YOU SHARE a concept or methodology that we are already using in our physical processes that can help us by adopting a similar way to improve communication?*

Mr. Onata: Jidoka. Have you heard of it? The concept of *jidoka* is often translated as autonomation, or automation with human intervention. The basis of jidoka is really about making sure everybody understands that if there is a defect in your process, you stop, seek the cause, and try to fix it immediately. The advantage of doing it immediately is that the root cause just happened, which is a good situation to be in. If the defect happened six weeks prior, it's very difficult to determine the root cause. So, it helps us highlight the root causes.

In an assembly line of components, when the operator finds a bad part, he or she stops the line immediately when the defect is found and finds a solution to the problem, or better yet, they kaizen. Everybody stops, and they try to figure out what happened and how they're going to prevent it from happening again. So, before I go into how to use jidoka for communication processes or how to think about it in the communication process, remember that communication precedes action; before anything gets done, you have a process of communication.

This is *why* we want to practice jidoka in our interactions.

Then, also remember that we're interdependent, and we interact as suppliers and customers. Instead of assembling components, we're assembling information, requests, and instructions.

Jidoka in communication then can be similar if we sense or detect a misunderstanding. When we suspect the meanings are not in common, it's our responsibility to stop immediately and start a dialogue with the other person. Bring the assumptions to the surface.

The assumptions become out loud assumptions, not hidden any more.

Realize that the idea or expectation is not in common. Take responsibility, and you have a chance to understand at the source, the root cause, why this just happened. Perhaps someone spoke too fast, perhaps the person is not a native English speaker, or maybe the instructions were not clear. Dialogue and clarify any assumptions until the meanings match and until you have a common understanding.

Better yet, kaizen together with others from your team, so everybody associated with your area understands what happened, because everybody can make the same mistake and have the same situation happen to them.

I'd like to share a story of what happened during a teleconference between colleagues inside the same company. People were sitting in Germany, while others were sitting in Detroit, Michigan, and the company's plant in Guadalajara, Mexico.

The discussion was about getting prototype parts delivered to the Detroit area. The German engineers pointed out the specifications of the prototype parts. They noted these were very fragile and therefore should be packaged a certain way to prevent them from breaking in shipping. In addition, the quality people who were in Detroit requested special labeling to ensure traceability.

This phone conference went on for about 40 minutes, and after everybody had their say, the team leader asked if everything was clear.

Everybody responded with a "yes."

Well, since I'm talking about communication, you can imagine that something did not go according to plan. In fact, the meanings were not in common, and the package that was received in Detroit looked more like a Chinese-food take-out box. And there was no traceability label present.

Unfortunately, when the package was opened, the parts inside were broken.

These were very important parts – small parts but critical for a very sizeable project. They had no way of making these parts again in time for the OEM's scheduled testing. The delivery dates were missed and, consequently, the OEM customer in Michigan cancelled their contract with this company.

Ladies and gentlemen, this cancellation cost the company $20 million. That's a lot of money! Even for me.

Obviously, the leadership was not happy. They needed to find out what happened, and, of course, they also wanted to avoid this from happening again. In order to avoid opinions or jumping to conclusions, they agreed to use systems-level cause analysis to find out what really happened – what had contributed to this $20 million contract loss?

The leadership also decided to assign the task of facilitating the investigation to the quality manager, who proceeded to establish a team from several areas of the organization. The quality training in this case called for cross-functional involvement to obtain the viewpoints from every area.

In the first meeting, "broken prototype" was initially designated as the nonconformance, and the first fishbone was filled out with the standard categories: people, methods, environment, measurement, machine, and materials.

Because of the distance separating the players from the United States, Germany, and Mexico, they proceeded to interview the people who had been on the teleconference and started to expose the issues that could have contributed to the problem.

As the interviews advanced, they realized that it had a lot to do with humans, technology, and misunderstandings. The meanings traded between the people sitting in Mexico and in Germany were not the same; there was a nonconformance in the meanings.

I also want to point out that when we are sitting face-to-face we have a clear advantage. For instance, if you see the person on the left saying, "Send me the prototypes," and the person on the right says, "Yes, no problem," when you're sitting close to someone, body language and facial expressions can point to whether the other person grasps your meaning, whether the expectation is 100% clear. These additional communication signals can help clarify and reduce the risk of ambiguity.

It's also easier to initiate a feedback loop for asking, for example, "What did you understand?" "What exactly is it that you're going to deliver?"

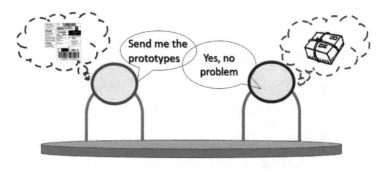

In a face-to-face interaction, the person on the left might sense that the "yes, no problem" is in fact a problem, and can initiate an exchange of meanings.

Unfortunately, face-to-face might be a wish, but this is not how many organizations function today. We don't live face-to-face anymore. Interdependence still exists, and it looks more like this.

The factor of distance represented in time zones, lack of face-to-face interaction, and the need to rely on telecom systems to interact impacts the communication process. When we cannot be seen, we think it's OK to multitask, which means we are not paying full attention to the meanings being exchanged.

Welcome to the real world. The new gemba.

We can have thousands of miles in between and multiple time zones. Often, we don't see who we are talking to, and all we hear are voices. Now, to make things more interesting, we have these IT devices, digital telephone systems that are supposed to convey our voices clearly. In my experience, on many of these international calls, voices are garbled. We have to really focus on what someone is saying because there is noise or static.

I've also experienced open microphones from other participants who are inside their noisy facility, and the background noise invades the conversation. Or we get disconnected. So, we lose our train of thought and experience more waste when we have to wait for IT to fix the issues and get reconnected.

I'm quite sure many people on the call were working on their laptops, replying to emails, writing new emails, multitasking, and not clearly focusing on what the other person was saying. On top of that, we have this device called the cell phone, receiving calls, texting others. Thus, more multitasking.

This lack of focus contributes to miscommunication because we are not really listening to each other. Our concentration gets diluted. Our attention is being drawn away from what someone is stating or presenting.

I call all of these competing signals "noise, they are signals that get in the way of the intended request or instruction, and you cannot listen to with your full attention.

In the case of our teleconference, the colleagues from Germany and the United States heard the other person say, "Yes, no problem," and took it for granted that things were going to get done right.

Going back to the misunderstood instructions, we're going to address three factors that contributed to the lost contract, starting with English. Some 5 Whys are shown to help illustrate.

In the West, English is the chosen language of business, but not everybody speaks it at the same level, and this actually had an impact on how people understood or misunderstood all of the instructions that were required to be successful, to obtain positive results.

In this case, we talked about English. Here is one of the paths we went down when we used the 5 Whys.

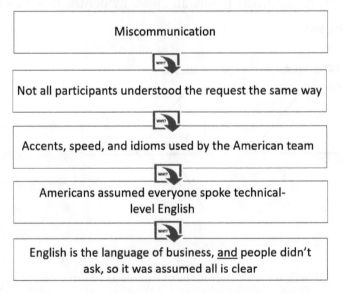

Example of a 5 Whys analysis related to the problem of English as the language of business.

We noted English as a contributor.

Why was there miscommunication? Because not all participants understood the requests the same way.

Why? Because accents, speeds, and idioms used by the American team confused some of the non-native English speakers.

Why did this happen? Because the Americans assumed that everybody spoke English with a higher technical level as required in our business environments.

Why? Because English is the language of business that was chosen. Plus, when people didn't ask questions, everyone assumed it was all clear. Evidently, this was not the case.

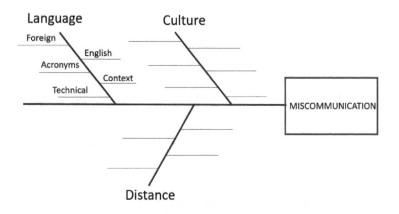

The branches show other potential root causes related to language.

Culture was another opportunity that was picked up on from the interviews.

Why was there miscommunication based on culture? Because not all participants understood the request the same way.

Why? Because they did not have a chance to ask questions.

Why? Well, they didn't want to sound stupid or lose face. Plus, the American team was rushing to conclude.

Why? Because saving face for some on the call was more important. Plus, "yes" was understood by the Americans and the Germans as confirmation that everybody was on the same page.

Why does this happen? Because cultural programming differences create different meanings.

That certainly was a big contributing factor in this situation.

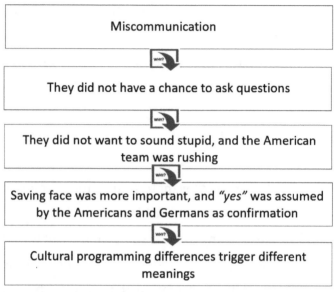

Example of a 5 Whys analysis related to cultural issues.

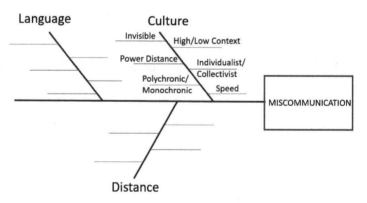

The branches show other potential cultural issues.

The third factor we will review is the environment, and I'm not going to discuss the environment as far as climate change or the weather. I talk about the environment as it relates to multitasking, an environment that creates a lot of noise and interference in the process of communication. That noise created a barrier to understanding.

Why did multitasking create or contribute to miscommunication? Because not all participants understood the requests the same way.

Why? Because they were not 100% focused on the details being discussed.

Why? Because they were distracted by emails and phone calls on their cell phones. Plus, because of IT issues, the communication on those telecom devices was not clear.

Why? Because multitasking is a standard way of working in this day and age. And, there were technical difficulties on the call because of the type of IT devices that were being used.

Why? Because "time is money" is regarded as the highest value, making it OK to be doing five things at once. And, they over-relied on technology to ensure communication was happening. In other words, they thought having these fancy devices to communicate with somebody else would help them understand things clearly.

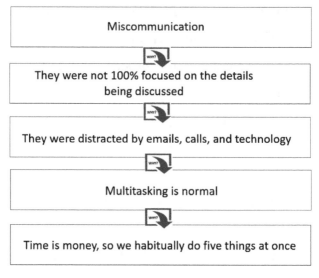

Example of a 5 Whys analysis related to multitasking.

Multitasking was also associated with the factor of distance, and they built some additional contributing causes:

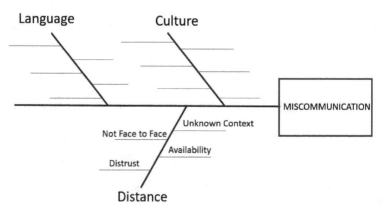

The branches show other potential causes related to distance.

By using the 5 Whys, the countermeasures were easier to determine. The organization's leadership was also satisfied because with a very simple methodology, facilitated by the quality manager, they avoided the typical blaming and opinions that in the past led nowhere.

There were certainly other factors that contributed to the problem; however, for the sake of simplicity, this slide summarizes the three sources, and to tie these directly to the associated countermeasures, they chose long and short term.

First, there was a meeting about ensuring English speakers were made responsible for speaking at a matching pace. That is, English speakers should use a slower pace when they know their counterparts and colleagues are from other parts of the world. Also, they must avoid using fancy language when there is no need to use idioms. If English speakers must use idioms, they should explain how these relate to the context. In addition, they should deliberately require people to give feedback. In other words, behave as customers and suppliers.

Second, global colleagues who did not have a good level of English, especially on the technical side, were engaged in classes to improve their skill level.

Third, they engaged the teams in several multicultural team trainings, mostly to raise the awareness of how people from other cultures behave, how they work, and how to work with them. Once again, the pillar of respect for people was brought into play.

Fourth, multitasking and cell phone use were flagged as sure ways to create problems. Telecom rules were established, and team leaders worked toward ensuring compliance.

Fifth, the IT department was challenged to improve the quality and reliability of the connections and the digital devices.

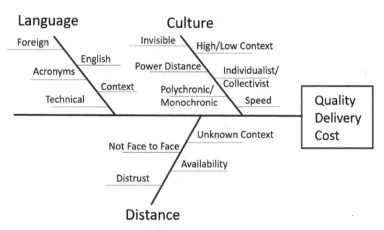

This fishbone shows the three factors together. These causes can be added to the typical shop-floor categories of man, machine, method, materials, measurement, and environment. If the fish is bigger today, perhaps it's time to make our fishbone diagrams bigger.

I think this section was intended to show a real case on how to use a simple quality tool to help dig deeper into real root causes associated with invisible factors.

If there are some questions, I will take them now.

Attendee 10: *That was a very eye-opening exercise, Mr. Onata. Would it be possible to expand on other issues contributing to the problem? What did the team learn so they could avoid future similar issues?*

Mr. Onata: Yes, it is worth mentioning something that was missed when they held the conference call. The call was scheduled as a regular meeting. This means there was no heightened level of importance set, nor was the criticality of the project mentioned.

If in the past some misunderstandings happened, they did not have a huge impact, and things were corrected somehow.

In this case, if they had made this an emergency meeting, perhaps adding a higher-level manager to explain why this had to be executed flawlessly, the attention paid to each detail might have been more complete, more focused.

So, the degree of importance and urgency might have stopped people from multitasking, causing people to pay real attention to the matter at hand.

One additional item they uncovered was that the list of open points or meeting minutes was assigned to the team in Michigan, so they were taking notes based on what they understood the agreement to be.

The team saw an opportunity to change this to a random method. Every meeting, someone would be chosen at random to do a verbal recap of the points they discussed and agreed to.

By choosing someone randomly at the conclusion of the meeting, people paid extra attention during the meeting AND asked questions for clarification. Only then would the meeting minutes be written based on the recap with better clarity. All ambiguity was removed.

And I have one last point. They saw another opportunity to create a "buddy" system, where each person was responsible for a direct relationship with a foreign counterpart. This would allow for a call after the call, to validate and certify the quality of the communication without creating a "loss of face."

OK, I suggest we take a short 10-minute break. When we return, I will share with you a few more real cases where the principles we have learned today have been put into action.

See you in a few minutes.

Mr. Onata illustrates a few cases

WELCOME BACK, LADIES AND GENTLEMEN. I would like to share with you how some teams have adopted this new gemba way of thinking and their successes. Perhaps, with these next cases, you too can think of a way to bring this into your organization.

The ideas are complementary to what your role is as quality and continuous improvement professionals, because our work has to match the current circumstances. Some of you are influenced by the way you have been taught by others regarding how to apply lean thinking or quality principles.

While it's quite possible it worked for your instructors and teachers in a few organizations, because it was OK in their circumstances, but it does not mean it will work in every case. Therefore, it is up to you to figure out the best way based on your current context and circumstances.

The new gemba means there are new types of waste and, therefore, we need new approaches.

Face to Face: The United States and the French

The first case I want to share is about a large OEM whose success depends heavily on its global tier 1 suppliers. It designs machines that are assembled from outsourced components. I will call the OEM Premium Machines Company, a U.S.-based enterprise.

Because of capacity constraints, Premium had to outsource to a company we will call France Tier 1 Group, since they were a French-based company. The outsourcing included sharing critical knowledge related to the material specifications and the physical transformation process.

For months, the teams from Premium and France Tier 1 thought they were communicating, because they had phone conference meetings on a weekly basis and follow-up emails. Unfortunately, ladies and gentlemen, they were suffering from the illusion we discussed earlier.

The team in France understood X while the OEM team intended Y. In addition, emails were often machine translated online and the meaning was interpreted.

Then, during a physical audit of the process at France Tier 1, the situation escalated quickly into a finger-pointing championship.

In the escalation, a top executive from the OEM, who was familiar with my work, contacted me. After a diagnostic assessment, a summit was designed.

The summit had one key advantage: it was to happen face to face, mainly because the diagnostic showed a key contributor to the situation was distance.

There were many great lessons from this summit, but I want to share that the teams from both organizations were meeting each other in person for the first time. What was accomplished in the first hour of the summit was worth more than $250,000 for the current project, and many millions after that.

All participants realized that their partners were not idiots, that they had the best intention to make each task of the project a success and, most important, that the problems were mostly related to the lack of relationship and trust.

How did they achieve the $250,000 benefit?

Once trust and respect were built, the teams were able to discuss in a transparent way how the physical process had been established. This is where an "aha moment" happened by the French team, who saw an opportunity to improve on the original intent and realize important cost savings.

The teams acknowledged the benefit of the face-to-face communication and also established ways to improve how they would communicate in the future, which of course became easier based on their newly formed personal relationships.

Face to face is like a poka-yoke that can avoid problems caused by distance. Do your teams use this poka-yoke?

Do you make a deliberate effort to meet face to face at the beginning of a project to establish a relationship?

Acronyms: Timeline confusion

This second story is about an averted production shutdown, through the use of mapping as a way to communicate.

I talked about acronyms as abbreviations that can create many problems, especially when not every interdependent participant in a supply chain knows what they stand for.

This was the case when the customer confused a major supplier by sending requests and instructions riddled with acronyms about schedules, specifications, and logistics. The customer in this case was a very large company with more than 30,000 employees who formed a tight-knit family and adopted their own lexicon to communicate.

Their abbreviated acronyms were originally intended to save time by not having to repeat long words for their processes and procedures. They got so accustomed to their use in day-to-day activities that they assumed everyone they talked with understood what they meant.

In addition to the confusion created by acronyms, the customer had strict holiday traditions to benefit its own employees, where it was OK to stop all work-related activities during extended breaks.

During a side conversation, one of the customer reps asked the supplier about some delivery details, which quickly sparked a crisis: because of the customer's holiday schedule and the misunderstood acronyms about timelines, deliveries would be missed and production brought to a halt.

It was not too late to recover some of the missed time. The two teams met and decided to clarify and remove ambiguity by using a visual map, showing the expectations in each step and what each corresponding acronym stood for.

The mapping showed a timeline gap of one month, for which multiple countermeasures were developed to avert a shutdown.

Later that year, I helped them set up and facilitate a work team to build a joint lexicon, one that would allow every player to be on the same page – a standard way to communicate.

Dr. Deming did talk about operational definitions in his book *Out of the Crisis*. "An operational definition is one that people can do business with ... must be communicable with the same meaning to vendor as to purchaser...." (Deming 1986)

Without such definitions there is no standard for understanding expectations. If everyone understands expectations differently, execution will surely happen all over the place.

Sounds a bit like uncontrolled variation to me.

How will you make sure your terms, internal lingo, and acronyms will be understood the same way by all stakeholders?

Meaning Lost in Translation: Design and specification changes

Continuous improvement sometimes creates opportunities for problems, which is what happened when the end customer needed specifications and dimensions changed on some automotive components.

AKMIE Motors, AG, a German-based company, translated its operations and supplier manuals into English for its suppliers to use as manufacturing guidelines. When their valve supplier filed a claim for $750,000 for obsolete components that could not be used for production, this sounded an alarm, and management got involved.

After a deep dive in the basis of the claim, it turned out that in the translation of the change management process, the words chosen in English to request information about a potential change were taken to mean: "we are requiring you to make the change," which drove a need to use different materials, making the older ones unusable and obsolete.

AKMIE was exploring a new process with new materials to reduce waste and improve the value to their customers.

While they were just asking for information about changes to costs and the possibility of delivery dates, the supplier assumed it was an instruction to proceed with the change.

When I was called to help out, I revisited AKMIE's process of translation, just like I once did for Boern Industries. In the case of AKMIE, the company had sent its manuals to translators who did not have an understanding of key processes and, therefore, chose words in English that did not support the intended meaning.

Plus, this was all done in batch – all manuals at one time with no allowance to do a PDCA cycle to involve the internal customers, the ones who would be executing based on the translation. No feedback loop, no learning. ([6])

AKMIE's supply chain suffered a $750,000 setback; big money lost in translation.

In this new gemba, where multiple languages are spoken, will you accept every translation as the true interpretation of the original meaning?

OK, let's take a short break of about 10 minutes. I will be outside to answer your questions.

When we return I will provide a summary for the conclusion of our conference.

"In times of change learners inherit the earth; while the learned find themselves beautifully equipped to deal with a world that no longer exists."

Eric Hoffer

Mr. Onata's Challenge

WELCOME BACK, LADIES AND GENTLEMEN. I enjoyed your questions and our conversations during the breaks. I spoke with engineers, and they understood what I spoke about in their terms. I spoke to supply chain personnel, and they too understood my talk in their own words, and I spoke to quality and continuous improvement professionals who understood my message from their own perspective.

Each of you is right, in your own unique way, and now it is important to realize how interdependent you really are on each other. This is the way our gemba is developing with all the outsourcing, supply chains, dispersed operations and teams made up of international folks.

If circumstances have changed and our gemba is different today, then shouldn't we shift the way we lead our quality and continuous improvement to grow and remain competitive?

We can no longer ignore the increased interdependence in today's business, along with the importance of what is happening beyond our four walls. Therefore, behaving based on the old reality is not going to get us anywhere good.

Please do learn from the past but remember to review the current context of the real place before applying stale countermeasures. Catch yourself in your programming so you can avoid following the "only way of doing things."

In addition, if our customer's expectations are a moving target with continuous change in tastes and wants, then we need to adapt to this new dynamic setting as our success can only happen through collaboration with the other stakeholders.

Communication with every business function, suppliers, customers, the community and governments has become a requirement to survive and thrive in this transformed gemba. We are in dire need of truly understanding each other's meanings before we can establish agreements to work in a coordinated way with each and every player involved.

So, this process of communication that we paid little attention to, and often delegated to Human Resources is now obvious that it is our responsibility. I would even call it the most important process of our times.

Before my summary, here are three illusions we need to stay more aware of in the new gemba:

We have covered many topics, so before we end our conference, I would like to summarize some key points to refresh your memory.

Please remember, my main goal for today was to raise awareness, to bring things to the surface that we will typically not see. Awareness creates a situation that we cannot completely forget something, and we cannot longer avoid taking on the responsibility to lead based on our new discoveries.

Gemba is a great place because it will not hide the facts on its own. But we might not always be looking for the facts. It's like those jumbled word games we play, where we have to find words inside a bunch of jumbled letters. The words are there, in plain sight, but our minds have to see things from different angles before we discover and *see* the hidden words.

This brings me to a few of the most relevant points of this presentation which I will enumerate for your benefit as a summary:

1. *Communication is invisible.* We cannot see it as it happens, but we can feel and measure its impact on our results. Communication is in itself an activity, and, therefore, we need to include it in our continuous improvement efforts. As I just mentioned, being aware of this will make it easier to continue to avoid or pretend it doesn't exist, or accept that a specific department is responsible for this process. This leads to the second point.

2. *Communication is a process.* In our case, it is a human process where two or more people are exchanging meanings with the goal of getting something done together. This factor is important because you have the skills to deal with processes, and, therefore, you can adapt those skills to drive improvement and quality into communication. Stated differently, misunderstandings that might cause unwanted costs can be reduced, potentially eliminating some of those costs.

   The human factor about this point is important, since there are also machine communications, IT systems that try to talk to each other, and sensory communication. But for our business goals, if we modify the process model from sender and receiver, to customer and supplier, there is a relationship created that carries expectations and responsibilities. The suppliers need to satisfy the customers, while the customers have to ensure their expectations are clear and unambiguous.

3. *Communication precedes action.* This point is about cause and effect, where bad communication can contribute to poor results in the new gemba. Because we are highly interdependent, before things get done, people have to communicate. This is true whether it's a project team, supply chain members, or different areas in your organization trying to coordinate a task. In a process, if one thing comes before another, it can influence the outcome of the previous step.

In a previous workshop, someone came up with an alternative way to say this: Communication "pre-seeds" action. The idea is the same. The seed of an action is going to greatly influence its results, just like the seed of a plant or a tree. If we know this, doesn't it make sense to deal with the seeds – the causes – so together we can find sustainable solutions?

If you are in agreement with points one, two, and three, then we can remind ourselves of the next point, number four:

4. *Communication is everyone's responsibility.* Just like quality. At every step of the value chain, we can have an impact on the final outcome. We cannot delegate this process because we are active participants in the process. We can be the cause of the effect. Even if we are not sending a message, we are receiving one, so we are responsible for listening, being curious, and asking. It is the quality of our interactions that will help us reduce the risk of costs associated with misunderstandings, and an interaction implies that more than one person is involved.

Taking responsibility for our participation in this process is directly associated with the word *respect*, which by the way is one of the key pillars for continuous improvement to be effective.

5. *Respect for people.* Anytime I bring up the word *respect* in my conferences or workshops, we have to discuss what it means. Yes, we can all assume everyone is on the same page about what it means,

which is just an assumption. And I will not dictate or prescribe what it should mean.

In the context of this conference, we are looking for successful outcomes for our team and our organization, so respect, in this case, is about ensuring clarity in our requests, our expectations, and the information we transfer to another person, to ensure the next task or activity will be performed correctly. We expect that the information we receive will do the same for us, right? Only once there is a shared understanding and meanings match can people execute their tasks and achieve the expected results.

If we want to be successful, we need to make sure our colleagues and partners are successful. Therefore, be sure to send clear, unambiguous instructions and requests to the next person so he or she can understand your intent and expectations.

If you are receiving an instruction, pay full attention, be curious about the message, and ask questions. That is also part of respect.

For me, respect means all people have a legitimate reason why they are set up the way they are, and why they work this or that way. If we can each feel respected, we will respect others in return.

Ladies and gentlemen, the opposite is also true. If we don't show respect, we will get push back. Also, people will not always be in front of you. Face to face is a luxury for teams. Therefore, don't assume "those guys" over there have a bad intention. They may live in different context and circumstances as you, but they have a legitimate right to think the way they do, and being different does not mean being better or worse.

If we accept responsibility for communication, we will at the same time respect the people we are interacting with, to ensure their success. Without getting into definitions of respect, we can at least see the reciprocity here: I need to respect to be respected. For your benefit, I would like to expand the summary with a few more key points from today's sessions:

6. *Go slow so you can move fast.* In the context of the new gemba, this is very important, because things are moving very quickly, and we may get dragged into communicating fast, without taking responsibility, without respecting our partners. This

point is especially valid when we have to interact with people we have never met, or people who live in a different part of the world. If we don't understand their circumstances, that is, the context they work and live in, they may interpret our ideas differently than we intended.

To go slow means to take time to establish a relationship first. It will be well worth the investment when misunderstandings can be avoided. Go slow means take time to dialogue until everyone is on the same page and understands the expectations, the instructions.

Make your assumptions out loud. Broadcast them as part of your dialogue process.

Once there is experience working together, speed will increase. But first we have to go slow.

7. *Zero defects, zero base.* This is more relevant today than ever before, because in the new gemba we are seeing an acceleration of problems related to human factors, such as communication. If we pretend to drive zero defects in our physical environments, we will need to include zero defects in our interactions. In the new gemba, effective interactions are exposed

to problems caused by language, culture, and distance. We need to grasp how to deal with these factors, which can be seen as new sources of variation that affect our results.

OK. I am very thankful for your participation today.

Please join me on this continuous improvement journey so we can together wear a new hat, lead and take on the responsibility for hidden factors, and discover new ways to stay ahead of the competition, especially in the invisible gemba.

Notes:

1. A few of my first books from the late 80's and 90's that served as a jumping board from the old Industrial Engineering curriculum into the work of Toyota's contributors:

   A Revolution in manufacturing: SMED (1985) by Shigeo Shingo Productivity Press, Zero Quality Control: Source Inspection and the Poka-Yoke System (1986) by Shigeo Shingo, Routledge; and One-Piece Flow: Cell Design for Transforming the Production Process (1992) by Kenichi Sekine, Productivity Press.

2. Story adapted from *Global Lean: Seeing the New Waste Rooted in Communication, Distance, and Culture*, by Sam Yankelevitch (New York: Taylor & Francis, 2016).

3. This is a commonly used quote by Dr. Deming for which I researched it's source and unfortunately could not establish it. In any case, it is very close

enough to Dr. Deming's philosophy and a widely used quote.

4. A great lesson from Daniel Kahneman's book: *Thinking, Fast and Slow* (New York: Farrar, Straus and Giroux, 2013).

5. SAP ERP is enterprise resource planning software developed by the German company SAP SE. SAP ERP incorporates the key business functions of an organization.

6. Examples of the use of PDCA are presented in *Lean Potion #9* and *Global Lean* (see References section of this book).

References

Bowie, David, and Brian Eno. 1977. *Heroes*. New York: RCA Records.

Deming. 1986. *Out of the Crisis*. Cambridge, MA: Massachusetts Institute of Technology.

Feigenbaum, A. V. 1983. *Total Quality Control*, third edition. New York: McGraw Hill.

Goldratt, E. M., and Jeff Cox. 1986. *The Goal: A Process of Ongoing Improvement*, revised edition. Great Barrington, MA: North River Press.

Imai, Masaaki. 1997. *Gemba Kaizen: A Commonsense Low-Cost Approach to Management*. New York: McGraw Hill.

Kang, Chang W., and Paul H. Kyam. 2012. *Basic Statistical Tools for Improving Quality*. New York: Wiley, 19.

MGM. 1939. *The Wizard of Oz*.

Milliken. 2017. *The Importance of Zero-Based Thinking.* Leadership blog. Spartanburg, SC: Milliken & Co. Available at: http://performancesolutionsbymilliken.com/ importance-zero-based-thinking/

Nakamuro, Jun. 2017. Re-translating lean from its origin. *LinkedIn Pulse* (January 4). Available at: https://www.linkedin.com/pulse/ re-translating-lean-from-its-origin-jun-nakamuro/

Online Etymology Dictionary. 2018. Available at: https://www.etymonline.com

Oxford Dictionaries. 2018. Available at: https://www. oxforddictionaries.com

Shingo, Shigeo. 1987. *The Sayings of Shigeo Shingo.* Portland, OR: Productivity Press.

Yankelevitch, Sam. 2014. *Lean Potion #9: Communication: The Next Lean Frontier.* Ashir Diss, LLC.

Yankelevitch, Sam. 2016. *Global Lean: Seeing the New Waste Rooted in Communication, Distance, and Culture.* Portland, OR: Productivity Press.